Escaping Hitler's Bunker

Escaping Hitler's Bunker

The Fate of the Third Reich's Leaders

Sjoerd J. de Boer

FRONTLINE BOOKS

First published in Great Britain in 2021 by
Frontline Books
An imprint of
Pen & Sword Books Ltd
Yorkshire – Philadelphia

Copyright © Sjoerd J. de Boer 2021

ISBN 978 1 52679 269 3

The right of Sjoerd J. de Boer to be identified as Author of this work has been
asserted by him in accordance with the Copyright, Designs and Patents Act 1988.

A CIP catalogue record for this book is
available from the British Library.

Typeset by Mac Style.
Printed and bound in India by Replika Press Pvt. Ltd.

MIX
Paper from
responsible sources
FSC® C016779

Pen & Sword Books Limited incorporates the imprints of Atlas, Archaeology,
Aviation, Discovery, Family History, Fiction, History, Maritime, Military,
Military Classics, Politics, Select, Transport, True Crime, Air World,
Frontline Publishing, Leo Cooper, Remember When, Seaforth Publishing, The
Praetorian Press, Wharncliffe Local History, Wharncliffe Transport, Wharncliffe
True Crime and White Owl.

For a complete list of Pen & Sword titles please contact

PEN & SWORD BOOKS LIMITED
47 Church Street, Barnsley, South Yorkshire, S70 2AS, England
E-mail: enquiries@pen-and-sword.co.uk
Website: www.pen-and-sword.co.uk

Or

PEN AND SWORD BOOKS
1950 Lawrence Rd, Havertown, PA 19083, USA
E-mail: Uspen-and-sword@casematepublishers.com
Website: www.penandswordbooks.com

Contents

Introduction

Through underground tunnels, crawling over barbed wire, swimming and rowing across rivers, by car, plane, on the back of a truck full of paintings or by foot. Many of Hitler's most noteworthy followers, who were still in the vicinity of the Führerbunker in Berlin at the end of the war, tried to escape the city in all sorts of ways.

This was quite difficult to achieve. The city was almost completely surrounded by the Soviet army, so getting away was a life-threatening operation and, just before Hitler's death, almost impossible. There had been better opportunities in the days right after the Führer's birthday on 20 April, ten days later, after Hitler's death, there was only one route still open: the route past the 'Weidendammer Brücke' across the River Spree.

Not everyone wanted to flee. Because Hitler was no longer alive and the Third Reich would soon cease to exist, Joseph and Magda Goebbels committed suicide, as did a number of army officers who remained in the grounds of the Reich Chancellery. But the majority of the people that were there did not want to die and tried to escape from a shelter that had become something akin to a prison for them.

Not only the prominent figures, such as ministers, civil servants and members of the armed forces, left Berlin. Secretaries, doctors and unknown boys of the Hitler Youth also wanted to leave the bunker area as quickly as possible.

Several eyewitness reports tell us how they tried to get away, and this book gives an overview of many of those accounts. In words and in pictures, the story of the escape of the most famous inhabitants of the bunker and the Chancellery during the last days of the 'Third Reich' is told here.

The story begins with the last ten days of Hitler's life and then follows the routes of those who fled. Some of the escapees did not see Germany for years because they ended up in a prison in Moscow, while others already in flight crossed paths several times. Many of them went to Flensburg, near the Danish border, where Admiral Dönitz managed to stretch out the Third Reich just a little longer. Others had left for the Obersalzberg or Bayern. Others tried to reach their families as soon as possible. An exciting highlight is the flight of a number of groups from the Chancellery's bunkers, at the very last moment, when men like Martin Bormann,

Artur Axmann, Wilhelm Mohnke and Rochus Misch used the final narrow metres of German territory to escape the city.

When it was all over, it was a long time before most of the signs of war disappeared from the city. Although many buildings, bridges and streets were reconstructed or replaced, numerous locations still bear the marks of the violence of war and the Third Reich. Not only in central Berlin, but also the airports, houses, villas, ruins and dilapidated military sites outside the city are reminders of that period. A lot of these locations are featured in this book.

Chapter 1

The Last Days Inside the Bunker

It's 30 April 1945. Hitler is dead. In his Berlin bunker, where he married Eva Braun the day before, there are not many people left. But in its vicinity there are all kinds of people: soldiers, guards, senior officers, party leaders, generals, secretaries, chamber servants and a large group of boys from the Hitler Youth. Many of them still want to flee the city, preferably to the west, towards the American and British armies. But the city centre, where the bunker is located, is surrounded by the Soviet army and there are only a few ways out of the city left.

Ten days earlier Hitler had turned 56. Telegrams and telephone calls with congratulations flooded in throughout the day and into the evening Propaganda

The main entrance to the ruined New Reich Chancellery, on Voßstraße. This picture was taken in July 1945, by British Lieutenant Frank Barnes of the 2nd Battalion Devonshire Regiment. (*Picture: James Luto Collection*)

A view of the Old Reich Chancellery and its modern extension, as seen from Wilhelmplatz, after the end of the war. Both the old and the new part of the Old Chancellery were badly damaged by bombing and the fighting in 1945. (*Picture: NARA*)

Minister Joseph Goebbels had praised him for his greatness in a radio speech.[1] While the city's airports were still accessible and a number of routes to the centre remained open, he proudly said that the Führer would never abandon his people, not even in these difficult times.

Several important party members and ministers visited the Führer that day. Even Hermann Göring, the man who devoted more time to his art collection and his addiction than on coordinating the air force. Heinrich Himmler, the SS leader responsible for the largest derailments of the empire inside the concentration camps, also paid a visit. Of course, Minister of Armaments Albert Speer, who after the war preferred to speak of his apolitical career as an architect than about his responsibility for the production of arms with which he had prolonged the war enormously, came to congratulate Hitler. In addition, there was Artur Axmann, the youth leader under whose command the young members of the Hitler Youth were sent to their deaths during the last days of the Third Reich. The Minister of Foreign Affairs, Joachim von Ribbentrop, who was scorned by many of his colleagues, also called

The New Chancellery was built along the entire left side of Voßstraße.

The Old Chancellery on Wilhelmstraße was in ruins after the war. New flats were constructed there much later, during the last years of the German Democratic Republic.

on the Führer as well as the fanatical Joseph Goebbels, who would be the last to abandon his Führer. Hitler's private secretary, Martin Bormann, had hardly ever left Hitler's side over the years.[2]

The building complex where Hitler spent his last days consisted of the Old Chancellery on Wilhelmstraße, which had also been used by previous German leaders, and the New Chancellery, which was built by Albert Speer. It ran along the entire length of the Voßstraße. On the corner of both streets an old building stood in between both parts of the Chancellery. Behind the buildings was an enormous garden, where the Führerbunker was. It wasn't the only bunker on the property. Right below the New Reich Chancellery was another one. The corridors and the cellars of the buildings and bunkers were connected to each other. From the New Chancellery, however, the Führerbunker was not freely accessible. In the corridor there were steel doors that were permanently guarded.

Hitler's Last Birthday (Friday, 20 April)

Inside the bunker, Hitler's birthday celebrations started just after midnight. It had been customary for many years for Hitler's personal staff to congratulate him, and so they were waiting for him in the hallway near his rooms. Hitler had

The rear entrance to the Führerbunker in the Reich Chancellery garden. The cone-shaped structure on the right was part of the ventilation system. It also served as a shelter for the guards. The square part of the building was an emergency exit from the bunker. The bodies of Hitler and Eva Braun were incinerated in the garden between the conical tower and the exit structure. (*Picture: Historic Military Press*)

Hitler's gardens lay behind both Chancelleries. The area was part of the no-go zone on the east side of the Berlin Wall and is now made up of offices, apartment buildings, car parks and a sports field.

indicated, however, that he saw no reason to celebrate his birthday and for a while it looked like General Wilhelm Burgdorf, Himmler's adjutant Hermann Fegelein, von Ribbentrop's adjutant Walter Hewel, press officer Heinz Lorenz and Hitler's adjutants Julius Schaub, Alwin-Broder Albrecht and Otto Günsche stood there in vain.[3] It was only when Eva Braun urged Hitler to go out there, that he opened the door so his followers could finally congratulate him.

Just a few moments later, the first military briefing of the day took place. Field Marshal Wilhelm Keitel, Admiral Karl Dönitz and Generals Alfred Jodl and Hans Krebs also congratulated their Führer after which the meeting began. At 0900 hours Hitler went to sleep, after he had instructed his chamberlain Heinz Linge not to wake him until 1400 hours.[4]

After breakfast Hitler made a brief appearance in the Chancellery garden, where he handed out medals to the Hitler Youth boys who had bravely fought against the Soviet army. Their leader Axmann was there, of course, together with

Goebbels, Himmler, Speer and Bormann. The young boys were lined up between the members of the recently founded army group 'Kurland' and the SS division 'Frundsberg'. Hitler walked in front of them, with a crooked back and trembling hands. He spoke a few short words and when he was finished, he muttered the well-known 'Heil'. But after his greeting, which was normally answered with a snappy 'Heil' back, everyone remained silent. Axmann said that the men must have been so impressed by the willpower of the Führer that they simply forgot to react.[5] Nobody knows if that was the real reason.

After the ceremony Göring and the other national leaders were waiting on the edge of the garden also to congratulate Hitler. After they had done this, Hitler went back inside the bunker for the next staff meeting. The military situation was dire. The Soviet army was so close to the German capital that the sound of their infantry could be heard inside the Reich Chancellery. The Allies from the West had already arrived at the River Elbe. Göring's chief of staff general Karl Koller therefore emphasized during the meeting that the Supreme Command of the Army had to be moved as soon as possible. And since Hitler was in command, the other attendees pointed out that, under these dangerous circumstances, Hitler had to leave for the south of Germany.[6] On the Obersalzberg, Hitler had a villa with a complete bunker complex underneath it. He would be much safer there, they said. But Hitler refused. He didn't want to leave his Berlin troops, he said.

Underneath this street and car park are the remnants of the foundations of the Führerbunker.

Farewell

After the meeting Göring spoke briefly with Hitler. Göring wanted to leave for the south, because, as he said, he would be able to command the air force much better from the Obersalzberg.[7] In addition, his hunting lodge, Carinhall, would soon fall into Russian hands, and his villa in Berlin, which was very close to the endangered bunker, so he had nowhere else to go than south. But there was little future for his air force. Hitler was already dissatisfied with Göring's performance and his ministry, but he let him go without paying much attention to it.[8]

Many of the other ministers, generals and civil servants now also left, because waiting any longer was far too risky for them. The best route to the south would probably remain open for just a few more hours and to the west one could still escape through the village of Nauen. Many of the important national socialists that were still in Berlin wanted to take a plane, which was very dangerous with all the artillery surrounding the city.[9]

But not everybody was allowed to leave. Several staff members, one of them being telephone operator Rochus Misch, stayed behind in the bunker. As long as there was a telephone connection with the outside world and Hitler was still alive, Misch had to do his work. But there wasn't that much to do anymore and while he was waiting between phone calls Misch had a lot of time to think. He began to wonder what was the point of all this waiting. Hitler's order to fight to the last man was meaningless if the German army only consisted of a few soldiers, some elderly men and a bunch of Hitler Youth boys. But as long as Misch wasn't relieved from his duties, he stayed in place, answering the phone and observing what took place inside the bunker.[10]

In the evening Hitler informed the members of his staff that they were allowed to go. His secretaries Johanna Wolf and Christa Schroeder were sent to the Obersalzberg. Adjutant Albert Bormann, Hitler's personal servant Wilhelm Arndt, photographer Walter Frentz, dentist Hugo Blaschke, security officers, press attachés and stenographers were also given permission to leave. Adjutant Karl-Jesko von Puttkamer was sent on a mission to the Obersalzberg. He had to burn important papers, which, for post-war historians, probably contained a wealth of information about the Third Reich.

From the courtyard of the Reich Chancellery men and women who were no longer needed departed in cars filled with suitcases containing valuables, clothes and all sorts of other things. They were driven to the Berlin airports of Gatow and Staaken. From there, until 23 April, four planes flew to Munich, Salzburg, Ainring and back about twenty times.[11]

Later in the evening secretary Traudl Junge sat in Hitler's office with a number of others. Hitler had always appreciated the company of the secretaries and had

Beyond this gate is the entrance to Hermann Göring's former Air Ministry. The building now serves as the Ministry of Finance.

The entrance to Göring's estate, Carinhall. Only some remains of the hunting lodge and the army buildings there can be seen today.

Berlin-Gatow airport is now an air force museum.

lunch with them every day, but that night he didn't speak much. When asked if he wanted to leave the city as well, he reacted negatively. He would force the decision of the battle in Berlin or go under. After saying that, he and his girlfriend Eva Braun went to his bedroom, leaving behind a group of people that had no hope of leaving the city together with their Führer. They could only wait and see what would happen.

A little later, Braun came back. She was still wearing the beautiful birthday dress that Hitler, according to Junge, had barely noticed. Braun wanted to party one more time and took everyone she met to the Führer's apartment inside the Old Chancellery. The table was set, music was playing, people drank and danced, because Braun wanted to 'dance, drink, forget . . .', said Junge. Even Martin Bormann and Hitler's private doctor Theodor Morell were there. Junge couldn't bring herself to enjoy the bizarre party. Nobody talked about their impending death, but, she said, 'here ghosts gave a party'. Junge left the room early and went out through the underground corridors to the New Reich Chancellery to go to bed.[12] The Führerbunker was almost empty at that time. Except for Misch, sitting by his phone, and Hitler, who was trying to sleep.

Hitler's Distrust (Saturday, 21 April)

The next morning Hitler's private assistant Heinz Linge woke up early to the sound of artillery fire. The Soviets had moved into the outskirts of Berlin and were now shooting directly at the city centre. That's why Linge decided to wake up Hitler at 0930, much earlier than he used to do. In the lower bunker, where Hitler slept, almost nothing was heard of the shelling, except when a grenade hit nearby.

Above ground, cars were still leaving the Reich Chancellery, on their way to an airport that was still functioning, transporting ministers Julius Dorpmüller (Traffic), Alfred Rosenberg (Eastern Occupied Territories), Bernhard Rust (Education), Ludwig 'Graf' Schwerin-von Krosigk (Finance), Franz Seldte (Labour), Otto Thierack (Justice) and Otto Meißner (head of the Presidential Chancellery) through the ruined city.[13]

Hitler seemed to derive some hope from the idea that General Felix Steiner's troops could march up to liberate Berlin, but at the same time he looked tired and depressed. He walked with difficulty, his hands trembled and it seemed as if his nerves were breaking down. His distrust of everything and everyone was getting worse and worse.[14] Air Force General Koller, who had gone back to his headquarters

The front door of Dr Morell's old practice located on Kurfürstendamm, a street now full of upmarket shops.

west of the city, got him on the phone. Hitler asked about what the planes stationed in the south could do to defend the city, but Koller had to explain that he did not know the answer because of limited communication at that time. Hitler hung up, but he called back a little later and said that he was surprised that the fighter jets, which were on an airfield in Prague, had not been used yet. After Koller explained that the jet planes could not be taken out of their shelter because there were too many enemy fighters in the air, Hitler became furious. He said he didn't need the air force anymore and yelled that its commanders had to be hanged immediately.[15]

Hitler also mistrusted his personal physician Theodor Morell. When Morell wanted to give Hitler his daily injection of glucose, Hitler reacted very suspiciously and shouted that Morell wanted to sedate him with morphine so the others could take him to the Obersalzberg. Morell did his best to convince him that it was the usual injection he wanted to give him, but Hitler sent him away and shouted that he could not be trusted. Morell went to his room, packed his bags and disappeared that same night.[16] He was very upset about Hitler's suspicion, and it seems he never got over it. Hitler stayed behind inside his bunker, his state of mind vacillating between severe depression and some last, unrealistic hope. To the outside world he persisted for a while, still believing that the Russians would suffer their greatest and bloodiest defeat at the gates of Berlin. There was no reason to believe that his hope was based on anything but hope itself.[17]

The Führer Collapses (Sunday, 22 April)

The Wilhelmplatz, in front of the Old Chancellery, was in ruins, just like the Hotel Kaiserhof had been for a year and a half now. Goebbels' nearby Ministry of Propaganda was also severely damaged. The Soviet army had reached 'Berlin-Gesundbrunnen', about 3 miles north of the bunker, and in the east of the city the Russians were also closing in. The problems Hitler had predicted between the Western Allies and the Soviets had not surfaced. Neither had Felix Steiner's attack to relieve Berlin. Steiner could hardly use the inexperienced men that he had left to save Hitler.[18]

The military briefings continued. Keitel, Jodl, Krebs and Burgdorf were present on Sunday, as were Bormann, Fegelein, Hewel and two other adjutants, Hans-Erich Voß and Eckhard Christian.[19] During the 1530 meeting, Hitler left the room twice, possibly because he was affected by all the bad news that came in. When he returned the second time, he asked everyone except Keitel, Jodl, Krebs and Burgdof to leave the room.[20]

Just outside the meeting room were Hitler's secretaries Junge, Gerda Christian and Martin Bormann's secretary Else Krüger. They must have seen some of the

The luxurious Hotel Kaiserhof, where Hitler often stayed before becoming Chancellor, was located here. It lay in ruins by the end of the war.

men come out of the room, after which the door was closed. They couldn't fail to hear the sound of loud voices coming from behind the door. Adjutant Schaub, who was nearby, later claimed that he had heard Hitler's booming voice coming from the map room.[21] Hitler made a 30-minute thunderous speech about the betrayal and cowardice of the army and the SS. He refused to go on like this because he was misled by his generals, he yelled. Fighting didn't make any sense anymore. Hitler collapsed, took a seat and said in a soft voice that the war was lost. He still wouldn't leave Berlin, but since he wasn't able to fight, he would kill himself at the very last moment. If there were to be negotiations, Göring had to take charge, because Hitler would never negotiate. Keitel and Jodl tried to convince him one more time that he should not lose hope, but it didn't matter anymore. Hitler had admitted that he would lose the war.[22]

Following this, Hitler left the meeting and went to his bunker room. After a while Hitler asked Linge to summon his secretaries Junge and Christian as well as his cook Constanze Manziarly. When they arrived, Eva Braun was present too. Hitler told them that a plane would soon leave and that the ladies were free to board it, because everything was lost anyway. When nobody reacted, Braun walked up to him, grabbed his hands and said that he knew she would stay with him and that she wouldn't be sent away. Then, Hitler kissed Braun on her mouth in front

A good part of the Ministry of Propaganda building is still standing. Behind the renovated facade, an older looking wing surrounds a courtyard.

of the secretaries for the first time. The emotional scene in this absurd situation confused Junge so much that she spontaneously said something she didn't really mean: she too would stay with Hitler in the bunker. The other two women also rejected Hitler's offer.[23]

Rochus Misch had received a similar offer for his wife and young daughter. He himself had to stay, but his family had a seat reserved on a plane that was headed to the south. Misch rushed home, but when he got there, he discovered that his daughter had a fever, so his wife was forced to decline the offer. She stayed in Berlin too.

Misch returned to the bunker where he heard that Hitler had just said that the war was lost and that nobody owed him anything anymore. For a moment Misch hoped he could leave too. But his chief Franz Schädle told him that they still needed a telephone operator inside the bunker. Meanwhile, the plane on which Misch's wife and daughter had been due to travel took off. In their place was Hitler's servant Willy Arndt.[24]

Back in his room, Misch received phone calls from Dönitz and Himmler who both tried to persuade Hitler to leave Berlin, but Hitler didn't listen to them either. Von Ribbentrop took the trouble to come to the bunker himself to persuade him to leave, but he wasn't even admitted to Hitler. Hitler only wanted to see Goebbels. At about 1700 hours he called him and repeated his complaint about the betrayal and cowardice of the army. Goebbels came to the bunker as soon as possible and spoke in private with the Führer, which seemed to calm him down. Hitler even asked if Goebbels wanted to come to the bunker with his family.[25]

The Exodus Continues

Now that the city was almost surrounded and Hitler had pronounced the situation hopeless, the army's headquarters could not remain in the city centre, if only because of the inadequate and ever-failing communications. However, Hitler was commander-in-chief of the army and he had no intention of leaving the bunker. Jodl had already made sure that one part of the Supreme Command went to Berchtesgaden, but it soon moved to the nearby area of the Königssee, because of the threat of air strikes.[26] The other part of the Supreme Command of the Army would go to Krampnitz, near Potsdam. Hitler remained at the helm and important decisions still went through him.[27] But while the military briefings in the bunker continued as usual, they became less frequent and took place with far fewer staff members.

After this important decision Keitel left for the headquarters of General Walther Wenck's Twelfth Army. Wenck had to stop his defence against the Americans

The mountains by the Königssee. Jodl moved his headquarters from Berchtesgaden to a village further away, to avoid possible air raids.

Schönau am Königssee is a village near the Obersalzberg. Hitler often visited this restaurant near Lake Königssee or took a boat trip across the lake from this location.

south-west of Berlin and head for the city instead, in a new attempt to relieve it.[28] But even Wenck's army was no longer up to this task. The *force majeure* he would have to face was far too great.

Meanwhile, the exodus continued. Dozens of crates containing stenographic reports of staff meetings were carried upstairs and many people were getting ready to leave. Sergeant Julius Schaub was ordered to burn papers from Hitler's room in the Chancellery garden.[29] Then he had to do the same with Hitler's personal documents in Munich and on the Obersalzberg. As the military briefings became less important, the last two stenographers, Kurt Haagen and Gerhard Herrgesell, also departed by plane.[30]

In addition to the remaining secretaries, kitchen staff, housekeeping staff, telephone operators and drivers, Nicolaus von Below, Otto Günsche, Heinz Lorenz and Heinz Linge were still present. Occasionally the dreaded Obergruppenführer 'Gestapo-Müller' also walked through the building. Goebbels and his wife and children now came to stay at the Führerbunker too. They took rooms inside the upper bunker, one floor above Hitler's rooms. Goebbels had a room next to Misch's switchboard. Misch did not know it then, but after the war he learned that the plane that his wife and daughter could have taken had crashed near Dresden, probably shot down by the British army. Willy Arndt, who replaced the two, was dead. But Misch's family was still alive in Berlin and survived the war.[31]

A Telegram from Göring and a Visit from Speer (Monday, 23 April)

The atmosphere inside the bunker and the Reich Chancellery was steadily deteriorating. People stayed in their rooms or walked around aimlessly, waiting for news from outside or for Hitler's final decision. The fixed daily rhythm of the place eventually completely disappeared. There was much talk of death and suicide and the explosions were getting closer, but Hitler's mood had cleared a bit, compared with the day before. On this new Monday he even went into the garden for a while. It would be his last time outside the bunker.

The two secretaries who were still present stayed close to Hitler, but, like everyone else, they were waiting for some decisive moment. Joseph Goebbels, with his secretary of state Werner Naumann and his adjutant Günther Schwägermann, was still generating propaganda and collectively they decided that it would be good for the people to know that Hitler continued to lead his troops in Berlin, even under these extremely difficult circumstances.[32]

But there wasn't much left to lead anymore, so Hitler's suspicion, stirred up by his secretary Bormann, was getting worse. When Hermann Göring sent a telegram stating that Göring would have to take over leadership if he hadn't heard from

Hitler by 2200 hours, Hitler, at first, hardly reacted, although Bormann interpreted the message quite negatively and presented it as if Göring was giving Hitler an ultimatum. That was not necessarily true. General Koller had flown from the surroundings of Berlin to the Obersalzberg the day before and he had told Göring about Hitler's suicide plans. Because Göring was officially Hitler's successor, the question arose of when that succession came into effect. In view of the Soviet

Of the little that remains of architect Albert Speer's work in Berlin, his street lamps are the most striking.

Charlottenburger Chaussee, where many of Speer's street lamps had to be removed in order to allow aeroplanes to land near the Führerbunker.

encirclement of the city and the increasingly poor communications, the telegram was quite conceivably a request for a sign of life, in which Göring even stated that he hoped that Hitler would still be able to come to the south.[33]

Later, Bormann came with another telegram from Göring in which he asked Joachim von Ribbentrop to come to him as well. With this Bormann stirred up Hitler's suspicion in such a way that they both concluded that Göring had betrayed Hitler, and that there might even be a conspiracy against him. For a self-appointed genius such as Adolf Hitler, betrayal and conspiracies were a good excuse for his failure. He seemed to have forgotten that it was him who wrote in *Mein Kampf* that autocrats were preferable to a parliament, because they were personally accountable for their failures instead of some vague majority.[34] And now the time had come to take responsibility for the total collapse of the Third Reich, Hitler did nothing but blame others. Although he had said he wanted to hang the entire air force command, he spared Göring. If Göring resigned from all his duties, he would be arrested but he would not receive the death penalty. After Göring was informed of this, SS guards came to his mountain villa to make sure he did not leave his house.

Albert Speer returned to the bunker that day. He had driven a car from the north of the country in direction of Berlin. Near the city he took a plane which landed close to the Brandenburg Gate. The Tempelhof and Gatow airports were now under Soviet fire and therefore the lamp posts of the Charlottenburger Chaussee that Speer had designed himself were removed to convert the street into a runway. Speer landed between the Siegessäule and the Brandenburg Gate, not far from the Reich Chancellery grounds.[35] From there he walked to the bunker, where Speer wanted to say goodbye to Hitler.

Several accounts of Speer's last visit depict it as an emotional farewell, but it is difficult to say if that was really true. Hitler and Speer met behind closed doors and Speer contradicted himself about it after the war. He even claimed that he had considered killing Hitler by letting gas run into the bunker complex. Exactly when he had those thoughts and what the plans consisted of has never been made clear, and Speer was much less reliable than how people came to view him after the war. Speer, like many others, attempted to clean up his reputation when it was all over and distanced himself as much as possible from Hitler and his extreme ideaology.[36] After midnight Speer also visited Eva Braun in her room. He remained there until about 0300 and when Hitler entered the room, Speer said goodbye and left the bunker.

An Impossible Job (Tuesday, 24 April)

There weren't that many people that had really lived inside the bunker. Adolf Hitler and Eva Braun were there, of course. In addition, there were the Goebbels family, Dr Ludwig Stumpfegger, Constanze Manziarly and the adjutants Günther Schwägermann, Heinz Linge and Otto Günsche. Rochus Misch sometimes slept inside the bunker. He had a mattress in the telephone room, but he also had a room elsewhere on the premises, just like the other staff members. In the cellar under the New Reich Chancellery, a temporary hospital had been set up where Dr Werner Haase operated on and treated wounded soldiers.

Helmuth Weidling visited the bunker on Tuesday. He was an important general during the defence of Berlin and he had previously reported to the bunker to account for moving a command post from West Berlin to Döberitz, outside the city. According to Hitler, he should have been shot for that, but Weidling managed to resolve the misunderstanding. When he met Hitler again, he saw a man whom he later described as 'sick to death'. Hitler's leg and arm were shaking uncontrollably. When Weidling entered, it took Hitler a lot of effort to get up. Even after the Führer had shaken his hand and sat down again, his leg kept moving. Now Weidling had come again from his command post at the Bendlerstraße Hitler had a surprise for him. His opinion about the general had shifted completely and he appointed Weidling as commander in charge of the defence of Berlin.[37]

It was an impossible job. The access to Tempelhof airport was now completely blocked and Gatow was still under fire. This made the supply of ammunition even

After the failed attempt on Adolf Hitler's life in 1944, Claus Schenk von Stauffenberg, among others, was executed in the courtyard of the Bendlerblock, seen here.

Tempelhof airport also played an important role in Berlin after the war, for example, during the Soviet Union's blockade of West Berlin.

more impossible than it already was. As a successor to Göring had to be appointed, Hitler now ordered air force officer Robert Ritter von Greim to make the extremely dangerous journey to the bunker.[38] Outside the city, the Soviet army had surrounded the Ninth Army, the army that was to help Wenck's troops liberate Berlin.[39]

Communication with the outside world became increasingly difficult, so at times it was unclear where the Soviet army was. Misch therefore contacted random civilians who still had a connection, asking whether they had seen Soviet soldiers. If Hitler wanted to be sure he was in time to commit suicide, he had to know where the Soviets were.

Occasionally, the opposite happened and people in the city called the switchboard of the Chancellery as the number was listed in the Berlin phone book. Sometimes citizens were simply trying, just like operator Misch did, to determine where the Russians were, but at times shocking phone calls came in as well. On one occasion Misch had a woman on the line who was completely overcome with panick – her neighbour was being raped at that moment and Misch could hear the woman's screams in the background. Shocked, he passed the receiver to Goebbels.[40]

Worse than Reality (Wednesday, 25 April)

Over night the Chancellery was heavily shelled and when the sun rose the next morning the city centre was still under heavy fire. Berlin was almost completely surrounded. Fleeing to the Obersalzberg became definitively impossible during the morning when more than 300 American bombers spread their deadly cargo over the mountain. Hitler yet drew some hope from the position of the already encircled Ninth Army. It had been able to move towards Potsdam, a little closer to Berlin. He said that the situation in Berlin looked worse than it really was. But at the same time, near the River Elbe, the American and Soviet troops met and Hitler's prediction that these two powers would fly straight into each other's hair, came to nothing. Hitler and his men were trapped in a bunker which was fanatically defended by an army that was no longer functioning and by an air force without enough planes.[41]

In the city centre the atmosphere among Hitler's followers sank to an even lower point, when even the women inside the bunker discussed how to commit suicide. A shot through the mouth was best, Hitler advised them. But Eva Braun didn't like the idea of what that would do to her body. She wanted to be a beautiful corpse so she would take poison. The secretaries now also received an ampoule of cyanide. There was only one thing left they were waiting for, and that was Hitler's death.[42]

An aerial photograph of the Obersalzberg. Hitler's Berghof was located where there are now trees at the centre bottom of this photograph, just behind the road. (*Tom Zandt-Valentine*)

Göring's Successor (Thursday, 26 April)

Despite the constant shelling of the city centre, von Greim, who had been ordered to come to Berlin two days earlier, managed to land on the broken runway of Gatow airport. From there he took a smaller plane that could land in the city and flew it onto the Charlottenburger Chaussee. On the last stretch he was wounded, but because he had the famous aviator Hanna Reitsch with him, he survived. She was able to take over the controls to land the plane near the Brandenburg Gate. They requisitioned a car and drove through the ruins to Hitler's bunker. Supported by Reitsch, von Greim arrived at the Reich Chancellery, where he was treated immediately in the emergency hospital. Then the duo went inside the Führerbunker. Now that Göring had been deposed, a successor needed to be appointed. So, while Hanna Reitsch tried to persuade Mrs Goebbels to let the children go with them on their return flight, von Greim was appointed by Hitler as Field Marshal and Commander-in-Chief of the Air Force.[43] Hitler could very well have done that over the phone.

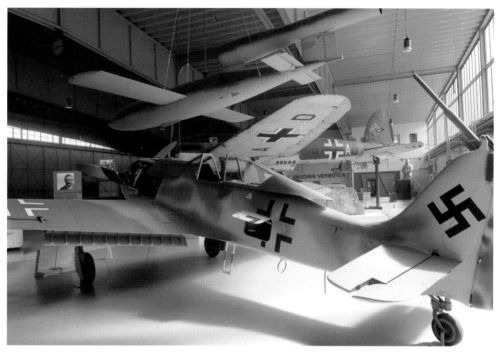

A Focke-Wulf Fw 190 A8 fighter plane at the museum at Berlin-Gatow airport. Behind it is an example of the V1. These flying bombs were frequently fired at London.

Another Betrayal? (Friday, 27 April)

During this last week inside the bunker the days merged together, with no clear boundary. Long sleepless nights ended somewhere in the new morning of a day that looked like the day before, Rochus Misch described.[44] That must have been true for Hitler too. He always went to sleep late and didn't wake up until late in the morning. But now the nights started to become very short. The enemy was so close that Hitler complained about the noise he could hear from the explosions close to the bunker. That noise, he said, prevented him from sleeping very well.

The first military meeting on Friday took place right after midnight. Krebs, Goebbels, Axmann, Weidling, Voß, von Below and Mohnke were present. These briefings had become increasingly pointless and troops were moved here and there without anybody knowing how strong they were or whether they still actually existed. The meeting at midnight was mainly about Wenck's men. Now that he had reached the outskirts of Potsdam, the hope he would enter Berlin was revived, but without reinforcements Wenck would never manage to reach the bunker. Hitler knew that and pointed out that he was not in Potsdam but at the Potsdamer Platz in the centre of Berlin.[45] After the meeting Hitler tried to get some sleep. He didn't want to be woken until the Soviets stood at his bedside, he said.[46]

Potsdamer Platz was very close to Hitler's Reich Chancellery, with the result that not much of the square was left standing after the war. The square was only rebuilt after the Berlin Wall fell in 1989.

Hermann Fegelein, Himmler's adjutant, lived in one of the flats in this building.

Later that day, when it appeared that Wenck had been forced back to the south of Potsdam, Weidling suggested once more that Hitler might still be able to get out of the city, if they broke through the Soviet front line and went to Potsdam themselves. But Hitler refused again. Together with the news that the first Soviet tanks had already been seen on the Wilhelmplatz, everybody realized that it would not be long before the enemy stood in front of the bunker entrance.[47] The tanks had been forced to withdraw but it was completely clear that if Wenck wasn't supported within 24 hours, it would be too late. Bormann drew the conclusion that there was no way out anymore and he wrote in his diary that they would endure and perish together with the Führer, faithful to the end.[48] But a few days later, when he had the choice between dying alongside Hitler and fleeing, he chose the latter.

On the same day someone noticed that Himmler's adjutant, Hermann Fegelein, had not been attending recent military meetings. Secretary Traudl Junge knew that he had called Eva Braun, who was his sister-in-law, the night before to persuade her to flee the city, but Braun had declined.[49] When Fegelein could no longer be reached by phone, members of the Reichssicherheitsdienst (RSD) were sent out to find him. In his house near the Kurfürstendamm they found him, drunk, in civilian clothes, or, according to others, without any clothes at all, together with a woman that was not his wife. A suitcase containing a large amount of foreign currency was also found inside his room.

When the men from the RSD returned to the bunker and reported back to Bormann, they didn't have Fegelein with them. Bormann then shouted that they had to go straight back to arrest him, even though he had a higher rank than they did.[50] When Fegelein finally arrived he was immediately demoted and secured in a room within the bunker under the New Reich Chancellery.[51] The next day, he'd have to appear before an improvised military court.

Hitler's Will (Saturday, 28 April)

The military briefings in the bunker's staff room became quite strange. There was simply no chance that help would come from outside the city and there was so little ammunition left that fighting would soon become impossible. Nevertheless, during the first meeting of Saturday, 28 April a telephone call went out to Keitel and Jodl, in which they received the absurd order that Berlin should be an 'absolute priority'.[52] Nobody knew what this meant. Didn't Berlin have that kind of priority before? With the Soviets so close, everybody knew that hope was an illusion and that the end would become reality very soon.

Hitler and Bormann's suspicions were again fed to the maximum when several reports came in about negotiations between SS leader Heinrich Himmler and a count from Sweden who was in contact with the Western Allies. Through him Himmler had made the Western Allies an offer to surrender, which was resolutely rejected because the Western and Eastern Allies had agreed they would only go ahead with Germany's complete surrender on both sides of the front. Himmler did not intend negotiating peace with the Soviet Union.

Hitler had left the matter for what it was, but when confirmation was received that betrayal, which had been going on for two months, had taken place, Hitler became furious again. He retreated, together with Goebbels and Bormann, to his own room where the three of them consulted extensively. Then Hitler sent for Fegelein. Himmler's adjutant must have been aware of Himmler's plans, Hitler shouted and Fegelein's suitcase filled with foreign currency didn't help him. After Hitler was done with him, Fegelein was handed over to a provisional court-martial that was only allowed to pass the death sentence. Fegelein was executed that same night.[53]

Just before midnight, Ritter von Greim was summoned by Hitler. He was ordered to leave the city to see to it that the air force would finally support the defence of

On the other side of this lake, the Suhrer See, were the temporary headquarters of Admiral Karl Dönitz.

Berlin. But probably just as important as this order was Hitler's revenge. Von Greim had to go to Plön, in the north of Germany, where Admiral Dönitz was. There he had to make sure that Himmler was arrested or killed immediately. Although the aviators preferred to stay at Hitler's side, they obeyed the order and were taken in an armoured vehicle to the Brandenburg Gate, where a plane was waiting for them. They miraculously succeeded in taking off through the shelling, but both orders were never carried out. There was too little left of the air force to help Berlin and just before the final defeat of Germany, Dönitz was no longer willing to execute Himmler.[54]

Shortly before dawn, Hitler located his secretary Traudl Junge and took her with him to a room where he could dictate some text to her. As she entered the room Junge saw a group of people come into the bunker, including Goebbels and the remaining generals. She wondered why they were there and why there was a table set inside the room, but she had to turn her attention to the Führer. Hitler immediately started dictating what turned out to be his political and personal wills. The former consisted of a not very innovative self-justification, an indictment of the Jews together with a section in which Hitler extensively arranged his succession. When Hitler dictated his private will after that, Junge discovered why the table was set and why guests had arrived. Hitler was to marry Eva Braun.[55]

A Doomed Wedding (Sunday, 29 April)

Immediately after Hitler had finished dictating, the wedding took place. Hitler rewarded Braun's loyalty with a marriage he had never wanted before. Bormann and Goebbels acted as witnesses. Magda Goebbels, the two remaining secretaries, the generals Krebs and Burgdorf, Commander von Below and cook Manziarly were the guests. Notary Walter Wagner, an employee of the Ministry of Propaganda, was driven to the Chancellery to conduct the ceremony. Hitler was dressed in a uniform and Braun in a beautiful silk dress. Within 10 minutes, the couple was married. A select group of people were invited to Hitler's study to toast the couple with a glass of Sekt.[56]

It was 0230 hours when Junge began typing out her notes in triplicate, so Hitler's will could be taken to three different locations. While she worked, Hitler kept entering the room to ask if she was almost ready. When he knew Junge had finished, Hitler retreated and went to bed. But Joseph Goebbels wanted to dictate something as well. He was emotional, because he and his wife had decided to die together with Hitler. To be able to do that he had to ignore Hitler's last order to leave the city and lead the government after his death. Apparently, he was struggling with that.[57] It was already morning, when the three copies of Hitler's will were finally signed. They were given to adjutant Wilhelm Zander, press secretary Heinz Lorenz and adjutant Willy Johannmeyer, who had to deliver them to the agreed locations.[58]

Goebbels' former Ministry of Propaganda now houses the Ministry of Social Affairs and Employment.

Pointless Missions

The attack on the last area of Berlin had begun. The Alexanderplatz, in the east, was in Russian hands. It was about 2 miles from the bunker. The Tiergarten, only 440yd away, was also under fire from the Soviets. The Potsdamer Platz, about 380yd from the location of Hitler's wedding, was already crawling with Soviet soldiers. Inside the bunker people were talking about suicide and Dr Stumpfegger continued to distribute ampoules of acid to anyone who did not have a gun.[59]

Not everyone gave in just like that. There were a lot of temporary occupants of the Führerbunker who wanted to leave, even before Hitler's death. Three of these were Krebs' adjutant Bernd Freytag von Loringhoven, Krebs' orderly officer Gerhard Boldt and Burgdorf's adjutant Rudolf Weiss. Whether the reason they gave for leaving was real or not, they managed to get permission to leave from Hitler himself. During the briefing at 1330 hours they asked him if they could try to break through to General Wenck's army so they could contribute to the

The Berlin Fernsehturm, television tower, was one of the city's most famous symbols of communism during the Cold War. It stands near Alexanderplatz, from where the Soviet army marched towards the Führerbunker.

liberation of Berlin. Hitler agreed and asked them to greet Wenck, but to tell him he had to hurry up.[60] Hitler's adjutant von Below also wanted to leave, so he asked Hitler for permission to break through to the west. Once more Hitler agreed, after which von Below left late in the evening with a letter for Keitel.[61]

Artur Axmann, however, took the opposite route. His post was in West Berlin, but it had become unusable. From his headquarters at the Kaiserdamm he had sent a large group of Hitler Youth boys into battle to prevent passage to the Reich Chancellery. A lot of them were killed. But as the Soviet army moved further and further into the centre during these last days, Axmann was transferred to the Party Chancellery opposite the Old Reich Chancellery.[62] There he and his young untrained soldiers could continue fighting. His new headquarters were within a hundred yards of the garden of the Führerbunker.

From these headquarters, boys of the Hitler Youth defended the city centre against the advancing Soviet army.

Inside the chancellery Dr Haase had been ordered to test the poison ampoules, which had been officially handed out under Himmler's responsibility. Hitler now distrusted everything that had something to do with Himmler. Together with dog trainer Fritz Tornow, Haase was going to kill Hitler's dog Blondi with an ampoule. The dog died right after he bit through it. Hitler came into the room to look at the result. He left when he saw that the dog had died. Blondi's five puppies were shot in the garden.[63]

The Last Briefing (Monday, 30 April)

On 30 April 1945, at 0230 hours, Hitler wanted to say goodbye to the group of twenty to twenty-five guards and servants who were still with him. He spoke to them of betrayal and suicide and expressed the hope that they wouldn't fall into Russian hands. He hoped that they would be able to reach the British or American armies in time. SS guard Maximilian Kölz and SS waiter Erwin Jakubek heard it and testified about it. In addition to a number of staff members mentioned earlier, Hitler's personal co-pilot Georg Betz and SS guard Helmut Beermann also said

The Reichstag had not been used by parliament since it burned down in 1933. Nevertheless, heavy fighting took place in and around the building.

Berlin's town hall was also taken by the Soviets.

Even though the Soviet army had already reached Friedrichstraße, the route via the station still seemed to offer a possible means of escape.

goodbye to their leader. Shortly afterwards it was time for the medical staff, led by Haase and SS physician Ernst Günther Schenck, to say goodbye. In the course of the following day Hitler also saw Joseph and Magda Goebbels, Bormann, Burgdorf, Krebs, RSD chief Johan Rattenhuber, Peter Högl, Mohnke, Voß, Stumpfegger, Naumann, Hewel, Manziarly and Schädle for the last time.[64]

The final briefing took place at about noon. Weidling hurried from his post in the Bendlerstraße to the bunker. The Reichstag was already stormed and so was the Rote Rathaus in the east. In the north the Soviets had reached the Friedrichstraße station. Weidling predicted that the battle would probably be over by nightfall. The ammunition had by this point more or less run out and there was absolutely no supply from the air. Hitler decided that the groups that wanted to flee were only allowed to do so the next day, and only after the ammunition had completely run out.[65]

After the meeting Hitler decided it was time for him to die. He therefore summoned Otto Günsche, who had to make sure that his body was burned completely according to the instructions Hitler would give him. The Führer didn't want his corpse to be taken to Moscow as a trophy. Günsche called driver Erich Kempka and asked him to arrange for the supply of enough petrol to burn the corpses of Adolf and Eva Hitler.[66]

After lunch Hitler said goodbye to his secretaries. Junge said that Hitler looked at her, but that he didn't really see her anymore. Eva Hitler, who had given Junge one of her expensive coats, did. She told Junge to flee to the south, and to give her regards to Bavaria, since Junge came from the same part of Germany as Eva. When Hitler had said farewell to Bormann, Joseph and Magda Goebbels, Burgdorf and Krebs, he left for his study.[67]

At about 1500 hours Rochus Misch heard Hitler mumbling in the hallway. He spoke with Günsche, Goebbels, Linge and Bormann, but from his room Misch could not hear what Hitler said. When he looked into the hallway, he saw him disappear into his room. Eva followed him. Günsche closed the door and told Misch that Hitler didn't want to be disturbed.

Everybody inside the lower bunker was waiting. No shot was heard, but after some time chamberlain Heinz Linge was called. Linge, being Hitler's valet, was the designated person to open the door. Misch, who heard what was going on, walked into the corridor and saw Linge go in. After Linge opened the first door, he had to open a second door to get to Hitler. Misch did his best to look inside and when the door was opened far enough, he could see inside the small room. He saw Eva lying on the couch with her legs raised. Next to her, on the same couch or on the chair that stood right next to it, was Hitler. Both Adolf and Eva were dead. Hitler had shot himself through the head and Eve had bitten through an ampoule. Hitler's head hung forward, his eyes staring into space.[68]

Hitler's body was laid on the ground and wrapped in a blanket. As his servants carried him down the hallway to the stairs, only his shoes were visible. The corpses of both Eva and Adolf Hitler were taken to the garden where they were burned.[69]

Hitler's Ministers

None of the following ministers visited Hitler during the last ten days, but they did leave the city during that period. Minister of Transport Julius Dorpmüller (1869–1945) died in 1945 after a serious illness. Minister of Labour Franz Seldte (1882–1947) died two years later. The Minister of Education Bernhard Rust (1883–1945) and the Minister of Justice Otto Georg Thierack (1889–1946) committed suicide. Reich commissioner of the occupied Eastern territories Alfred Rosenberg (1893–1946) was sentenced to death. Ludwig 'Graf' Schwerin-von Krosigk (1887–1977) from the Ministry of Finance lived on for years after the war. He was imprisoned for some time, but was released in 1951. The head of the Presidential Chancellery Otto Meißner (1880–1953) was acquitted during the so-called Wilhelmstraße trials.

Chapter 2

After Hitler Died

Following Hitler's death, everyone was in a hurry. Günsche, who had arranged for the corpses to be set on fire in the garden, didn't even go back to check if they had burned completely. Neither did Linge. Most men were hastily making plans to break out of the Reich Chancellery. Others prepared to end their lives just like Adolf and Eva Hitler had done.

Erich Mansfeld was one of the guards in the garden area. In the afternoon he had noticed from his watchtower that there was something going on near the emergency exit of the bunker. When he went there to check out what was happening, he witnessed the corpses of Adolf and Eva Hitler being laid in front of the exit. After that Goebbels, Bormann, Günsche, Linge, Stumpfegger and Hitler's chauffeur Erich Kempka paid their respects.[1] Mansfeld and two other guards, Hermann Karnau and Harry Mengershausen, had observed the corpses burning outside or had seen the charred remains of Adolf and Eva.[2]

The bunker had been closed for half a day, but now Hitler was dead, the secretaries and other temporary residents came back to the bunker through the underground corridors of the Chancellery. Several of them walked to the emergency exit to look at the burning bodies. Telephone operator Rochus Misch did not. He was in the switchboard room and felt no need to take a look because he had already seen the bodies of Adolf and Eva inside the bunker. He was scared and wanted to leave, but he still did not have permission to go.

In the meantime, people gathered in the hallway near the switchboard room. Joseph Goebbels and General Mohnke were among them. They came into his room because they wanted to contact the Russians by telephone. That turned out to be a difficult task. A technician had to be sent to the Soviets in order to put in place a working telephone line. When he finally succeeded, Misch heard a Russian voice on the other end of the line. Quickly he passed the phone to General Krebs, who spoke excellent Russian.[3] With that, the final negotiations of the Battle of Berlin had begun.

A Quick Funeral

When the fire in the garden was extinguished, the remains of the Hitlers still had to be buried. It is not clear who gave the order to do so. It could have been RSD chief Rattenhuber.[4] Equally, it might well have been Günsche himself as he asked the two members of Hitler's bodyguard, Ewald Lindhoff and Hans Reisser, to bury the bodies in the garden, which Lindhoff confirmed. He said the bodies were charred and in a terrible state. Reisser didn't even have to help in the end, but he was the one who reported to Günsche that Lindhoff had taken care of everything.[5] It's possible Rattenhuber was involved in some kind of way with the disposal of the bodies.

Different points of view, different versions of several stories, different chaotic statements about time were recorded about these last days in the Reich Chancellery grounds. This provoked various conspiracy theories that have almost always remained impossible to prove. Nevertheless, they continued to appear until long after the war had ended, especially in the West. This was because many of the direct witnesses had died, been removed to Russia or had simply disappeared. It was a long time before the statements of important witnesses like Günsche and Linge,

The remains of Adolf and Eva Hitler were later brought to this location in Berlin-Buch, where a pathology clinic was located.

After the Hitlers' remains were examined, they were temporarily buried in the clinic's garden.

who were imprisoned in the Soviet Union until the mid-1950s, were released. Of course, this hampered uncovering the truth about what happened to Hitler, and to such a degree that it still seemed necessary in 2018 for a French scientist to re-examine Hitler's remains. Needless to say, it was concluded that Hitler had committed suicide.[6]

Negotiations (Tuesday, 1 May)

On the night of 30 April/1 May, General Krebs and his adjutant Theodor von Dufving crossed the front line between the Führerbunker and Anhalter station. After having made contact with the Soviet Command, General Mohnke had escorted the two men to the crossing point, where Krebs was expected at the Hotel Excelsior, opposite the station. Mohnke, from the other side of a barricade that was put up, could see that a Russian officer was waiting for the two men.[7] They

Berlin's Anhalter station, a key location, was bombed several times during the war. This is the only part of it that remains.

were taken to the hotel and from there to General Vasily Chuikov, probably at his headquarters on the Schulenburgring, near Tempelhof airport.[8] Krebs told Chuikov that Hitler had committed suicide and handed him a letter from Bormann and Goebbels. Now Chuikov knew Hitler was dead, he made direct contact with Joseph Stalin. He told him what Krebs had said about Hitler and mentioned Krebs' proposed armistice.

It took a long time for Krebs to get back to the bunker. Stalin, who, like the Americans, did not want a unilateral peace, had rejected the German request and after that the negotiations stopped. The Soviets gave the Germans until 1600 hours to issue a declaration of complete surrender.[9] Otherwise the battle would continue until the bitter end.

At the time Krebs met Chuikov, Dönitz did not know that Hitler had died, although the Führer had appointed him as his successor. Bormann and Goebbels did not inform him of the Führer's death until the attempt to negotiate with

The entrance to General Chuikov's headquarters, near Tempelhof airport.

The staircase behind the front door leading to the flat where Chuikov once received Krebs. On 2 May, General Weidling signed the order to surrender Berlin here.

the Russians had failed, and that meant that they had tried to negotiate without consulting him. Bormann had sent Dönitz a telegram, but it only said that Dönitz, who had already moved into his northern headquarters Forelle near Plön, would be Hitler's successor. Dönitz even wrote a message back to 'Mein Führer' in which he declared his unfailing loyalty to him.[10]

At the end of the morning of 1 May, Dönitz finally received a message revealing Hitler's death. It was not until 2226 hours that Dönitz made a radio broadcast announcing that the Führer had fallen during the Battle of Berlin. It had taken more than a day for the army and the German people to be informed of Hitler's death, and still his suicide wasn't mentioned.[11]

Family Drama

Meanwhile, inside the bunker the most awful drama had taken place. In the early evening, Goebbels and his wife had spent some time together near the telephone exchange manned by Rochus Misch. The children were also present and Magda Goebbels combed their hair before taking them to their room at the front of bunker on the floor above. After that, it became quiet in the lower bunker, Misch said, and it took a while before Misch saw Magda Goebbels coming back. She was on her own, now. From the telephone room he saw her sitting in an adjoining room, where she grabbed a pack of playing cards and began a game of solitaire. Then she started crying.[12]

The inhabitants of the bunker must have known something about what had happened to Goebbels' children, but it turned out that no one could testify about what exactly had taken place. Except for SS dentist Helmut Kunz. Everyone else who was inside the children's bedroom that evening would commit suicide. Kunz stated that he anaesthetized the children with morphine. Then Magda Goebbels stayed with them until they slipped into unconsciousness. After that, Kunz said, she and Dr Stumpfegger put a lethal ampoule between the children's teeth, then one of the adults pressed their jaws together.[13] No one talked about it, but it was obvious something terrible had happened. When Misch saw Magda Goebbels crying over her playing cards, all six of the Goebbels children were already dead. Magda herself was given an injection of something to calm her nerves. Misch did not know whether or not Joseph Goebbels had been with his children when they died.

Already Angels

Magda Goebbels didn't have to live very long with the thought that she had killed her own children because she and her husband had decided to commit suicide right after the children had gone. Magda went back into the children's bedroom to see them one more time, after which she and her husband said goodbye to Naumann, Schwägermann and driver Alfred Rach. Coincidentally, as the couple went up the stairs to the emergency exit, General Mohnke entered the bunker. He came up behind them and said to Joseph Goebbels, 'Mr Secretary of State, we are going to break out. I want to say farewell.'[14]

Joseph and Magda turned around and spoke with Mohnke. Magda told him that their children were already angels and that their parents would soon follow them.[15] After that, while several men holding cannisters of petrol stood in the hallway ready to set fire to their corpses, the Propaganda Minister and his wife left the bunker for the garden.[16] When Joseph and Magda Goebbels had put an end to their lives, the soldiers went out, lit the bodies and left. No one buried anyone anymore.

At 2200 hours, Misch found the bodies of Krebs and Burgdorf inside the bunker. They had killed themselves with poison.[17] That must have been about the time of the Goebbels' suicide, but Misch had an alternative version of the story about the deaths of Joseph and Magda Goebbels. He said that after everyone had left, only he and mechanic Johannes Hentschel remained inside the bunker. Misch could now finally leave, but he was late and in a hurry to catch up with those who had already departed. After the war, when Misch finally met up with his friend again, the mechanic told him that Joseph and Magda Goebbels committed suicide within 5 minutes of Misch's departure. The difference about this compared with the other statements is that this must have been some time after midnight.[18] If he was right, though, it would suggest that the Goebbels didn't end their lives until 0355 hours on 2 May, 5 minutes after the latest possible time Misch exited the bunker. And there was more in Misch's statement that was remarkable. He said that Hentschel had told him that Magda and Joseph Goebbels killed themselves inside the bunker and not in the garden. Misch also didn't believe the Goebbels committed suicide together. Magda, he said, took her life in the children's bedroom, while Joseph killed himself in his study.[19] But Misch was the only 'witness' here and even he had only heard about the incident second-hand. Most of the other witnesses stated that the Goebbels died on 1 May. Since the people that fled the Chancellery grounds started leaving at about 1100 hours, Mohnke must have already said goodbye to Joseph and Magda Goebbels before that time. Most historians conclude that the Goebbels' suicide took place on 1 May. Their time of death might have been as early as 2030 hours, but was probably a little later, just before 2200 hours.[20]

Chapter 3

The Escape to the South

Many people left the Berlin government quarter during the last week of Hitler's life. Officials, secretaries, family members of Hitler's staff, they all wanted to get out of the city before it was too late. The Tempelhof, Gatow and Staaken airports were still open on 23 April and from there planes continued to fly back and forth to Salzburg and Munich. The south of the country, just like the northern part, was still not occupied by the Allied forces, so for the time being it was a good option to go there. Some of those who escaped went to the Berchtesgadener Land, where Hitler and other well-known party members

There is little left of Staaken airport, but this tower remains, now surrounded by business premises.

Salzburg, the destination of several flights from Berlin during the final days of the Third Reich.

had villas on the Obersalzberg. All kinds of fantasies arose about Hitler's last fortress there, but since Hitler had indicated that he would stay in Berlin, there was no real plan to defend the mountain. An all-encompassing battle on Hitler's mountain was out of the question if it was up to Hitler. But Martin Bormann had built an impressive system of corridors and bunkers inside the mountain and that meant that the Allied forces had to at least consider the possibility of Hitler hiding there.

Those who didn't go to the Obersalzberg area sought shelter in Bavaria or Austria, usually at their family homes. Some went into hiding. The army hierarchy, such as Air Force General Karl Koller, remained in post until the capitulation. Koller was eventually forced to move his headquarters to Austria.

The Mooslahnerkopf on the Obersalzberg, a viewpoint that Adolf Hitler often walked to from his Berghof.

All kinds of interconnected corridors and bunkers were constructed within the Obersalzberg.

Göring's Air Force

Hermann Göring, who was then still supreme commander of the air force, had had absolutely no intention of staying inside Hitler's bunker. He owned a beautiful house on the Obersalzberg and it seemed he still had some hope he could live there for a while. He had ensured that his enormous art collection, which he had collected at his hunting lodge Carinhall, was brought to the mountains near Berchtesgaden. Trainloads of artworks and other expensive things were transported to a tunnel there or to a bunker near the mountain.

A train full of art was hidden by Göring in this tunnel at the end of the war.

Just like Göring, Air Force General Karl Koller left Berlin on 20 April, but didn't go south immediately. After attending a briefing at the Führerbunker, he went to the headquarters of the Supreme Command of the air force at Wildpark-Werder, near Berlin, to coordinate what was left of the air force. It seemed that Koller's chief Göring no longer made useful contributions and from the Berlin bunker only strange telephone calls with unrealistic questions and orders from Hitler and Krebs were received concerning the deployment of the greatly reduced air force.

Inside the Führerbunker the air force had been under heavy verbal fire. This had been going on for quite a while, but after just a day Koller decided to relieve his representative Eckhard Christian whom he had sent to the bunker. It was impossible for an officer, Koller thought, to stand Bormann and Hitler's constant mocking of the air force for more than one day. And also on that day Christian witnessed Hitler's complete collapse. When Christian returned to the air force headquarters at about dinnertime, he informed Koller about it and explained that the army's Supreme Command, led by Keitel and Jodl, was now leaving the city. Concrete orders for the air force had not been given.

Christian and Koller concluded that given the military pressure on Berlin, combined with Hitler's desire to remain in the city, it had become impossible for

The Krampnitz barracks, which were taken over by the Soviet army after the war. These dilapidated buildings will soon be replaced with new housing.

Koller and his wife stayed at this hotel near Berchtesgaden. (*Ordercrazy, 2012*)

Those who wanted to go up the Obersalzberg had to pass this guardhouse first. There was another checkpoint close to Hitler's villa.

Hitler to lead the army. That was a logical conclusion: almost everybody left Berlin, except Hitler, while communication with the bunker was becoming increasingly difficult. If Hitler would leave with the army commanders, he could at least make decisions based on facts, they thought.

By then Göring had informed Koller that he was needed on the Obersalzberg, but Koller first wanted to speak with the Chief of Operations of the Supreme Command, Alfred Jodl. Jodl would at least have an overview of the situation of the army at that moment, Koller thought, and he probably felt that Göring couldn't help him with that. Therefore, Koller went to the army headquarters in Krampnitz where Jodl explained to him that the rest of the army command would arrive there soon. The army's strategy would be to negotiate with the Western Allies. Keitel and Jodl wanted to move as many troops as possible from the Western to the Eastern Front, without the German army being overrun in the West. The complicating factor was still Hitler's unwillingness to negotiate. After discussing this, Koller proposed to Jodl that he would fly south with some of his staff members and that Christian would join the Supreme Command in the north.

Göring's Dilemma

Jodl agreed to Koller's plan, and that meant that Koller could arrange his departure from his northern headquarters. He left with a plane from Gatow airport. From the sky he saw the ruins of a burning Berlin one more time. A few hours later he landed in Neubiberg, near Munich. On his way to Göring's villa he drove through the Bavarian village of Glonn, where he collected his wife. In Berchtesgaden he took her to the Hotel Haus Geiger and immediately drove on to Göring's villa on the mountain.[1] He didn't have time to eat or sleep.

Göring wanted to know if Hitler was still alive and whether he had already appointed Bormann as his successor or not. Koller could reassure him that Hitler had still been alive when he left, and that Bormann was not in command yet. Koller also advised Göring to send a message to Hitler, and this would become the famous message that Hitler and Bormann interpreted as Göring's treason.

Göring should act as soon as possible, Koller said, because according to his information Hitler was in such a predicament that he could hardly lead the army anymore. But Göring feared Bormann. 'If I act now', he said, 'they will call me a traitor, but if I wait, I will fail.' There was no way he could escape this dilemma, but because he was still Hitler's official deputy he had to do something. Koller suggested he write a message in which he proposed that he, Göring, should take over if Hitler wasn't able to react in time.

When Koller returned to the village of Berchtesgaden after the compilation of the message, he did not know what the outcome would be. After a short drive,

Koller was reunited with his wife at the hotel where he could finally sleep for a while. Later that evening it turned out that Göring could no longer be reached but nobody in the village below the Obersalzberg knew why.

During 24 April, it became clear to Koller that the message he had suggested had had the opposite effect to that which he had hoped for. Göring was arrested and not allowed to leave his mountain villa anymore. Koller being a high-ranking officer under Göring's command was now under fire too. In the morning, when he finally had time to eat some soup with his wife, he was disturbed by one of his men who entered the dining room. He told Koller there was an SS officer outside who wanted to speak to him. Koller asked if his officer could let the man in, but his officer hesitated because he was wary about the situation. He explained to Koller that the SS officer had not come alone, but with a group of armed SS men. It looked like they had come to arrest him. He advised Koller to crawl through the window to get away, but Koller refused to do so. He ordered his officer to let the SS officer in.

When the SS officer finally entered the room, he apologized for intruding and said that although he respected General Koller very much, he had been ordered to arrest him. Koller went along with it, but it wasn't long before his arrest was lifted. Ritter von Greim had become the new commander of Göring's air force and he couldn't do without Koller's expertise in this field.[2]

Frentz's Photo Archives

Photographer and cameraman Walter Frentz had also arrived at the Obersalzberg at about the time of Göring's arrest. He was an air force officer, who had worked with Leni Riefenstahl on her famous movies *Triumph des Willens* and *Olympia*. He had taken about 20,000 photographs during the Third Reich. It was Frentz, for example, who took the last pictures of Adolf Hitler meeting the boy soldiers in the garden of the Reich Chancellery on 20 March. On 23 or 24 April Frentz had boarded a plane with Albert Bormann that took them to Munich. After that, he had gone to the Obersalzberg by car.

Eva Braun had advised Frentz to hide his negatives inside the bunker under the Berghof, but fortunately he brought a large part of his work to a castle near Sigmaringen and to his parents' house in Bad Ischl. Frentz was arrested on the Obersalzberg, because he was an air force officer under Göring, but after having been taken to Salzburg, he was ordered to go back to the Berghof to hand over his negatives to the SS. After that, Frentz was free to go, but the Obersalzberg negatives have since disappeared.[3]

Ruins on the Obersalzberg

Göring's downfall reached the next stage when on April 25 the Allied bombers flew to the Obersalzberg to throw their lethal load on Hitler's fortress. Göring lived within a few hundred yards of the Berghof, which meant that his house was a target too. Since the cellar of his villa was connected to the bunker system, Göring, his wife and his daughter hurried to the entrance of the bunker. But when the first bombs had fallen, they still stood waiting in front of the bunker door because the SS guards kept the door locked. When the next batch of bombs was dropped, the guards decided they couldn't leave them standing there and permitted them to enter the mountain bunker after all.[4]

Of all the villas and buildings that had been constructed on the mountain during the Third Reich, few were left standing. Hitler's house had become unusable, the SS buildings were in ruins, of the kindergarten was nothing left but a pile of bricks and Bormann's house was also badly hit. The two hotels on the mountain were still standing and in reasonable order, but little was left of Göring's house, and therefore,

Hermann Göring's villa stood here. A new luxury hotel has been built to the right of the pond.

This is all that remains of Martin Bormann's villa.

despite his house arrest, he had to leave the Obersalzberg. Heinrich Himmler, as head of the SS, was forced to make this decision. He couldn't do much else but let him leave the mountain, although he did give Göring permission to choose for himself where he would like to go, albeit under the supervision of SS guards.

This building on the Obersalzberg was constructed by Martin Bormann as a guesthouse. It has been converted into an information centre on the history of Nazism.

A day after the Obersalzberg had been turned into a wasteland, Koller was summoned back to Berlin. From Schleißheim airport, near Munich, he flew back through Rechlin, but during the flight the situation in Berlin changed completely. It had become impossible to get into the city, Ritter von Greim told him over the phone. It was way too dangerous to come and moreover not very useful anymore, von Greim said. During the same conversation he asked Koller to keep supporting him, so Koller tried to get von Greim out of Berlin by sending several planes towards the city, but none of them arrived.[5] As his journey turned out to be pointless, Koller flew back from Rechlin to Neubiberg airport on 28 April. At the air force office on the Prinzregentenstraße in Munich, he arranged a car with which he drove back to Berchtesgaden.

To Austria

On 30 April, it appeared that Göring had left the Obersalzberg, although in the village below, Berchtesgaden, nobody seemed to know where he had gone. Some thought he had travelled to Salzburg, but in fact he had chosen to go to a castle in Mauterndorf, Austria. He had lived there as a boy with his mother and her lover. Later in life Göring had bought the property. He was taken in convoy with his wife and daughter to Mauterndorf.[6]

Mauterndorf Castle, Austria, owned by Göring and where he stayed for a short time at the end of the war. (*Klaas van der Wal*)

He had chosen a place where he felt at home and where he could still live in comfort. Here he received the news that Hitler was dead and knowing the Führer had gone, Göring's guards began to wonder what to do with him. They asked their superiors if they should keep him locked up or not.[7]

In the meantime, Koller tried to get Göring released from house arrest and called General Field Marshal Albert Kesselring about it, but he couldn't help him without first consulting Dönitz. Meanwhile, the Americans closed in, which meant that the Supreme Command of the army was moved to Zell am See in Austria, where it stayed at the so-called Thumersbach villas and hotels and Koller's Air Force Staff followed. Headquarters were made for him and his staff in a small medieval castle, which had been owned by the artist Thorak. It looked like a prison, Koller said. The Supreme Command soon retreated further south but Koller remained at Thumersbach, where he and his staff had not much more to do than wait for the Americans to show up.[8]

Consultation with Eisenhower

On 6 May Kesselring decided that there was little point in keeping Göring prisoner any longer and he ordered his release.[9] Göring immediately took advantage of this and sent a letter to Dwight D. Eisenhower in which he requested meeting. He thought that this could prevent further bloodshed, he wrote. Göring, who did not appear in Hitler's political will, apparently thought he still had something to say in the Third Reich.[10] In reply, the Allies suggested that a conversation would take place and they asked Göring to come to Fischhorn Castle, which was near Zell am See.

By the afternoon of 7 May it was quite certain that the Americans would arrive soon. General Alfred Jodl had already signed the documents of the German surrender, so Koller decided it was time to say goodbye to his staff, his soldiers and his officers. In the garden of Gasthof Nonnenhof, next to the castle in Thumersbach, he gave a short speech. He admitted that the war was over and that Germany had collapsed. He said to his people, 'We have done our best and we can stand before God and our people with a clear conscience.'[11] If Germany's enemies agreed with this, it had yet to be proven.

Fischhorn Castle, Austria, where Hermann Göring expected to meet Dwight D. Eisenhower. (*Klaas van der Wal*)

Waiting for Göring

In the meantime, Göring's successor Ritter von Greim had finally flown to Graz, Austria. When von Greim called on arrival, he didn't know anything about the capitulation of Germany. Koller told him that it was best for him to come to his headquarters, where he arrived the next morning. Hanna Reitsch was with him and he was still walking on crutches following his wounding over Berlin. The fanatical new leader of the air force had trouble believing that Germany had capitulated and he and Reitsch continued to cling to Hitler's ideas. Koller was no longer convinced by Hitler's doctrine and he said to both pilots that he thought the Führer had departed life a coward, after having completely destroyed the country. A lively discussion ensued that also covered Göring. Von Greim forbade Koller from helping him. Göring was a traitor, he said, and Reitsch, while crying, asked Koller not to do anything to support him. But Koller didn't understand their position. The Soviet army was coming in fast from the East and doing nothing meant that Göring would fall into their hands.

The American headquarters in Kitzbühel, where Hermann Göring stayed for a short time. (*Klaas van der Wal*)

Von Greim was in a hurry, also because the Americans were closing in. He wanted to leave quickly but Koller advised him to go to the hospital in Kitzbühel first. There, someone could take care of his injured leg. Koller explained that soon they wouldn't be able to travel anymore, because the Americans had indicated that they were going to prohibit German cars on the road. Koller ordered some of his men to accompany von Greim and Reitsch. He himself stayed behind, waiting for the Americans to show up.

When the two of them had left, a German major from Fischhorn Castle soon came to report that American Jeeps with officers had arrived at the castle and that they were waiting for Göring to appear. Eisenhower had not come with them. He had never intended to talk to Göring and instead he had sent General Robert I. Stack to meet him. But after the Americans had been waiting for a few hours, Göring didn't turn up either. The American general then became impatient and Koller decided to call Mauterndorf Castle where Göring was based to ask if he had already left. A staff member answered the phone. He told him Göring had set off at noon. As it was 1600 hours he should already have reached the castle, so the American general decided to drive towards him.

At about that time Koller received another call. It was from one of the officers that had accompanied von Greim. He relayed that south of St Johann von Greim had stopped the car and he and Reitsch had put on civilian clothes and planned to flee into the mountains, leaving their escorts behind. Koller told his subordinate that he thought that was a bad idea. Von Greim wouldn't get very far on crutches, even if Reitsch helped him, Koller said, and he ordered his officer to prevent them from doing so. If necessary, he said, the officer could suggest taking them to von Greim's staff at Elmau instead of bringing them to the hospital. That turned out to be an acceptable compromise for von Greim.[12]

Göring still had not arrived at the castle near Zell am See. He had suffered enormous delays in the traffic near Radstadt. But when General Stack arrived in that area it wasn't difficult to spot Göring's large car among all the other traffic. Under American escort the remainder of Göring's journey was a lot faster and he finally arrived at Fischhorn Castle.[13] But his role was over and Göring never got the chance to negotiate. Instead, he was taken to the American headquarters in Kitzbühel.

Koller was not arrested yet and he soon left Austria to return to the Berchtesgadener Land on the other side of the border. There, on 25 May, the Americans said that Eisenhower wanted to speak with him too, but Koller didn't meet with Eisenhower either. After he was allowed to say goodbye to his family and was then brought to an interrogation camp in Great Britain.[14]

Hermann Göring (1893–1946)

The Palace of Justice in Nuremberg. This is where leaders of the Third Reich, including Hermann Göring, were tried.

Reich marshal and Minister of Aviation Hermann Göring was flown from the American headquarters near Kitzbühel to stay in Augsburg. On 20 May 1945 he arrived at the Allied Interrogation Centre at Ashcan Camp in the Palace Hotel in Mondorf-les-Bains, Luxembourg. There the luxury that Göring was accustomed to came to an end. Together with fifty-two other senior Nazi officers and officials, including Dönitz, Keitel, Jodl, Robert Ley, Hans Frank, Alfred Rosenberg, Hjalmar Schacht and Julius Streicher, he stayed in a simple hotel room that was heavily guarded. A large quantity of pills were found in Göring's bag. According to the camp commander Colonel Burton C. Andrus, this was the largest collection of pills he had ever seen – 20,000 tablets of the heavy painkiller paracodeine. The number of pills Göring took per day was reduced under strict control. Göring had been dependent on these drugs for a large part of his life but was now free of the addiction. On 12 August 1945, Göring was taken to an airfield in Luxembourg City, together with fifteen of his fellow prisoners. From there the former airman took off for the last time and was flown to Nuremberg where he was placed in a prison right behind the Palace of Justice, where the famous Nuremberg trials took place. He was

Göring committed suicide in a cell in this prison.

sentenced to death, but on the evening before his execution he bit through a capsule of cyanide and died in his cell. His ashes were thrown into a tributary of the River Isar in Munich.

Karl Koller (1898–1951)

At the end of May, Air Force General Karl Koller returned from Austria to Strub, near Berchtesgaden, where he was arrested by the Americans. On 26 May his staff gathered outside his office to say goodbye before he was taken away. From Munich he was taken to the airport at Kaufbeuren. As a pilot he could see that his plane was not bringing him to Eisenhower. It landed north of London and Koller was brought to the British Interrogation Camp 7 in Oxford. In 1947 he was released. He returned to Germany.

Robert Ritter von Greim (1892–1945)

Successor of Göring and the last commander-in-chief of the air force, Robert Ritter von Greim was arrested by the Americans, who took him to a hospital in Salzburg because of his injuries. There he heard that the Americans would extradite him to the Soviets. On 24 May 1945 he committed suicide by biting through a poison capsule.

Hanna Reitsch (1912–79)

The famous German aviator Hanna Reitsch was arrested by the Americans together with von Greim. She spent eighteen months in various internment camps. She was interrogated extensively, especially about what she had experienced inside the Führerbunker. She was released in December 1947. She continued to fly for the rest of her life. In 1961 President John F. Kennedy invited her to the White House. She was buried in Salzburg.

Walter Frentz (1907–2004)

Photographer and filmmaker Walter Frentz went to his parents' house in Bad Ischl after he was released by the SS. After the capitulation of Germany, it is said he went to Stuttgart and Frankfurt am Main. In September 1945 he was taken to the Oberursel interrogation camp near Frankfurt. After he was released, he was arrested for a second time on 22 May 1946, after which he was locked up in the SS camp at Hammelburg. After his final release, he went back to work as a cameraman.

Hitler's Berghof

On board one of the first flights from Berlin to the south of Germany were Hitler's secretaries Christa Schroeder and Johanna Wolf. Hitler allowed them to leave on 20 April while his two younger secretaries had to stay behind. Hitler told Schroeder that he wanted to set up a resistance movement in Bavaria and that the two of them were more useful there than inside the bunker, Schroeder claimed. If Hitler really said that, it must have been a complimentary excuse and the second reason he gave seemed a lot more credible – the younger secretaries had a much better chance of getting out of the city if everything went wrong.

As part of their preparations for leaving, Schroeder and Wolf left the Führerbunker and went to the bunker under the New Reich Chancellery. While they were waiting for a signal, Hitler called. He told them that the road to the airport was temporarily impassable and that they had to wait until the next day before they could leave. But just after midnight he called again and said that they had to hurry because now there was a plane ready for departure.

The two secretaries speeded through the busy corridors of the Chancellery to the courtyard of the Radziwill Palace on the nearby Wilhelmstraße. There was a truck waiting for the luggage and another truck that was supposed to take them

The only parts of Hitler's mountain villa still visible are the foundations at the rear.

Some people, like secretary Schroeder, still called the Old Reich Chancellery the Radziwill Palais. Inside the building Hitler had a private apartment. At the end of the war trucks and cars were waiting in the courtyard there to take escapees and their luggage to the airfields. (*Picture: Bundesarchiv, Bild 146-1998-013-20A/CC-BY-SA 3.0*)

Hitler's secretaries arrived at Tempelhof airport by mistake, but were still able to leave for the south.

to their plane. It drove through the ruins along the pitch-black streets of Berlin to Tempelhof airport. A Ju52 airplane would be there to take them to Bavaria. But there was no plane of that type and the truck with the suitcases had not arrived either.

The airport commander found out that both the aircraft and the suitcases were at the Staaken airfield, but he advised them to board a transport plane at Tempelhof that was about to leave for Salzburg. They did and Hitler's secretaries landed safely in Salzburg. From there they were taken by bus to Hitler's villa Berghof on the Obersalzberg. They were lucky things went wrong, Schroeder later wrote, because the plane from Staaken they were supposed to take crashed near Dresden. It was the same plane that Misch's family would have taken if they had been able to.

Lucky Again

Karl-Jesko von Puttkamer also left the bunker on 21 April. When the secretaries arrived at the Berghof he was already destroying important papers of the Führer, as he had been ordered to do.[15] He had taken two non-commissioned officers with him to help with the job. When they had burned everything they had to, von Puttkamer left for Munich.

The closed passage to the bunker rooms of Adolf Hitler, Eva Braun and Theodor Morell within the tunnel system of the Obersalzberg. This is where Schroeder stayed after the bombing.

Hitler's apartment was on the second floor of this building in Prinzregentenplatz. Here Schaub destroyed all kinds of items belonging to Hitler.

Schroeder witnessed the SS officers taking over the mountain on 23 April, but at that time she did not know they had come to arrest Göring. The Berghof was also surrounded by SS men, but they did not interfere with Schroeder or Wolf, nor with Eva Braun's mother and sister who had been staying at the mountain villa for some time.

The secretaries were still on the mountain when it was bombed. When they heard the first explosions, they rushed downstairs where there was a passage to the bunkers underneath the villa. Something terrible could have happened, but the secretaries were lucky again. As soon as they had entered the bunker, a bomb fell directly on their bedrooms. Both rooms were destroyed just like the rest of the villa. Its walls were still standing, but the roof had been obliterated and there was rubble everywhere. Eva Braun's sister, Gretl Fegelein, left for Garmisch at once, but Schroeder had no idea where to go, so she spent the night in one of the bunker rooms.

Shortly after the bombardment, on 26 April, adjutant Julius Schaub appeared. He had been working with Hitler since the 1920s and had taken one of the last flights from Berlin to Munich. He had been a loyal servant of Hitler since he had participated in the failed NSDAP coup in 1923, and, just like Hitler, he had been imprisoned for it. In the 1940s, he became Hitler's personal adjutant, which obviously meant that Hitler trusted him. As a result, he had been ordered to destroy the last remaining papers and other belongings at Hitler's villa on the Obersalzberg. Most probably this task was not within von Puttkamer's remit and so Schaub now collected the items and burned them on the terrace of the Berghof. Schaub also got rid of a lot of material at Hitler's apartment in Munich.[16]

Plundering the Obersalzberg

Christa Schroeder had seen Schaub at the Berghof but she later wrote that he hardly spoke to her and that when he had finished he immediately disappeared to Berchtesgaden. Albert Bormann, who had left Berlin a few days after the secretaries, stayed there too, together with his wife. From the Hotel Berchtesgadener Hof he

The Hotel Berchtesgadener Hof, where Albert Bormann stayed, no longer exists. The centre for the surrounding national park now occupies the site.

The site of Bormann's model farm, which was looted by villagers.

arranged for groceries to be sent to the residents of the Berghof, so that they could stay there a little longer. It is possible Schaub stayed at the same hotel as Bormann.

When on 1 May Hitler's death was announced, villagers immediately stormed the model farm that Martin Bormann had had built on the mountain. Together with Albert Speer's house, that was also still standing, it was plundered. Animals, furniture and anything of any value were dragged down the mountain to the village. After a while strangers came to the Berghof too and they also snooped around the bunkers. Some policemen came to the complex inside the mountain to empty Eva

Both houses on this hill belonged to Albert Speer. He used the building on the right as his architect's studio and lived with his family in the property on the left.

Hitler-Braun's bunker room. They were ordered to take everything that referred to her, the police officers said, including Braun's photo albums and self-made films.

Schroeder's colleague Johanna Wolf had already gone to the town of Miesbach in Bavaria. She had said that she would investigate whether she and Schroeder could stay there with friends, but she never returned. Schroeder remained behind waiting to hear from for her but when Albert Bormann came to warn her that the Americans were approaching, she still hadn't had any contact with Wolf.[17]

Schroeder's Departure

Someone had arranged false papers for both secretaries, but when the papers arrived Schroeder was still alone and she decided it was time to leave the mountain. When a truck arrived to take the art from Hitler's villa to Austria, she helped to

Hintersee is the name of both the village and the lake where Schroeder ran into her old friends again.

identify the most expensive paintings. Then Schroeder took some valuables and a folder containing architectural sketches by Hitler and boarded the truck that was headed for Fischhorn Castle in Austria. But when the truck arrived in Hintersee, only a few miles from Berchtesgaden, she got off at the Hotel Post, where she met Bormann and Schaub again.[18] Albert Bormann and his family had moved to this hotel, but because he was afraid that he would be confused with his brother, he had planned to leave this new location soon. He hated his brother, and the two barely spoke if they were around each other. If one of the brothers told a joke at a packed table and everyone laughed at it, typically the other Bormann would not react. It was said that if Albert got a message meant for his brother, he would despatch an orderly to deliver it to his brother, even if they had adjoining rooms.[19] And now Albert had to leave because of his brother.

A number of other acquaintances of Schroeder, such as Hitler's dentist Hugo Blaschke and the wives and girlfriends of Dönitz, Linge, Schaub, Kempka and von Putkammer, also had rooms at the hotel. Some of them were accompanied by children or other family members.[20] Because Schroeder knew these people, she decided not to travel any further.

Bormann and Schaub did and not long after the truck with the paintings left, they were also gone, leaving their families behind.[21] Blaschke remained at the hotel. As a dentist he didn't fear the Americans much.[22] His assistant Käthe Heusermann was still in Berlin.[23]

Hitler's Train

Schaub might have had another assignment near Zell am See, Austria, where he first joined the army's command. His other job involved Hitler's special train, which was located at nearby Mallnitz. There, Schaub had to see to it that the train was destroyed.[24]

Another source states that this probably took place at another location in Austria and that the train was still in some kind of use on the south side of the Tauern Tunnel, near Mallnitz. It wasn't destroyed there though, but in Saalfelden, in the north. And there, only the Führerwagon was blown up, while other parts of the train were spared.

In conclusion, it is possible that Schaub was involved with the destruction of the Führerwagon at one of the above-mentioned locations, but he couldn't have destroyed the entire train. According to *After the Battle* magazine, the rest of the train was taken over by the US army. Later on, it was given back to the German Bundesbahn company. The president of West Germany still used Hitler's sleeper carriage in the 1970s.[25]

Schroeder and the other guests at the hotel knew that they could not stay there forever, but it took until 22 May 1945 when an officer of the American military intelligence entered the hotel. He was looking for Albert Bormann.

After the remaining guests told him Bormann was long gone, the officer wanted to know who they were, which meant that Schroeder had to identify herself too. Whether her false papers gave her away or if she decided to identify herself is not clear, but she was taken to the office of the intelligence service in Berchtesgaden that same afternoon.

Six days later Schroeder was taken by car to the so-called Bärensiedlung, a neighbourhood with small houses built for the staff of the Messerschmidt company in Augsburg. There she met Schaub again together with Hitler's famous photographer Heinrich Hoffmann. Schroeder was there for four days of questioning, during which time her suitcase was checked by an officer who discovered the paintings she had taken from the Berghof. Because she told him that the folder with the sketches of Hitler belonged to her father, she was allowed to keep them, but she never saw Hitler's paintings again.

Christa Schroeder (1908–84)

Hitler's secretary Emilie Christine Schroeder was imprisoned in various camps after the war. Following the interrogations in Augsburg, where she also met her colleague Wolf again, she was transported to the Mannheim-Seckenheim camp and after that some barracks in Fürth. At the end of September 1945 she ended up in the Nuremberg prison. She acted as a witness during the Nuremberg trials. In November of that same year she moved to Lager Hersbruck. It is possible that Johanna Wolf was also sent there.

In May 1946 Schroeder was brought to Kaserne Ludwigsburg, where she shared a room with Heinrich Himmler's wife and daughter. In November 1946 she met Hitler's driver Erich Kempka at the American City Hospital in Ludwigsburg. He had been admitted there following a car accident and remained there for a few months. After Schroeder was released on 12 May 1948 she lived in Munich.

Johanna Wolf (1900–85)

It turned out that secretary Johanna Wolf, after she had left Schroeder, moved in with her mother in the village of Bad Tölz, about 7½ miles from Miesbach. She was arrested there on 23 May 1945 by the American Intelligence Service and was taken to the same camp in Augsburg where Schroeder was. Johanna Wolf was released on 14 January 1948, a few months earlier than Schroeder. She spent the rest of her life in Bavaria.

Karl-Jesko von Puttkamer (1900–81)

Hitler's adjutant Karl-Jesko von Puttkamer had survived the famous von Stauffenberg attack on Hitler's life on 20 July 1944. Little is known about his whereabouts after he left the Obersalzberg, but he seems to have gone to Munich. The historian Trevor-Roper wrote that there von Puttkamer received a telegram from Martin Bormann on 28 April. It contained a strange and desperate message. Bormann wrote that the commanders of the army kept silent instead of ordering their troops to relieve Berlin. 'Treachery,' Bormann wrote, 'seems to have replaced loyalty. We remain here', he continued. 'The Chancellery is already in ruins.' Von Puttkamer was arrested and detained in May 1945. He was released on 12 May 1947. He died in Munich in 1981 and was buried at the Waldfriedhof there.

Julius Gregor Schaub (1898–1967)

Adjutant Julius Schaub left Hintersee for Zell am See where he used false papers in the name of 'Josef Huber'. In spite of that he was arrested on 8 May 1945 in Kitzbühel. He was imprisoned in various internment camps until February 1949, including the Bärensiedlung at the end of May 1945. There he met secretary Schroeder again. After his release he lived in Munich.

Albert Bormann (1902–89)

After Reichstag member Albert Bormann left Hintersee, he may have gone to the Bavarian countryside and worked on a farm near Forsting. Others say he went to the Austrian area of Pongau, right across the border. At some point maybe his family even joined him there. If that is correct, it must have been in the area of Saalfelden, Austria. Bormann used the surname 'Roth' as an alias. It could be that both stories are true because Bormann didn't get caught until 1949, when he finally turned himself in. He was questioned at the so-called Hauptspruchkammer, an organization that was responsible for the denazification of Germany. Albert Bormann was forced to work in a labour camp for six months. After that he stayed in southern Germany until he died in Munich in April 1989.

Hugo Johannes Blaschke (1881–1959)

Hitler's dentist Hugo Blaschke must have left the Hintersee hotel well before 22 May when the intelligence service took in Christa Schroeder and the others. Blaschke himself was arrested on 20 May 1945 in Dorfgastein, Austria. The American Intelligence Service interrogated him, focusing on Hitler's teeth. Later Blaschke described Martin Bormann's teeth and this was used to identify his remains in 1972. Blaschke was interrogated as a witness during the Nuremberg trials, after which he was transferred from the Nuremberg prison to the internment camp Nürnberg-Langwasser in December 1947. There he was initially sentenced to three years in a labour camp, but was released in December 1948. Blaschke continued to practise his profession in Nuremberg.

Crying Over Hitler

Hitler's personal physician Theodor Morell had always followed Hitler everywhere and he thought that the Führer had always appreciated him. The doctor had treated Hitler in his own unique way, which earned him a lot of criticism from his colleagues. But Hitler had always protected his doctor against them. At the end of the war, Morell was sick. He suffered with heart disease and cerebral oedema which made it difficult for him to go up and down the bunker's stairway when Hitler needed his daily injections. But he was always there.

When Morell had come to the bunker on 23 April to give Hitler his daily injection, he was shocked when Hitler declared him crazy and started shouting at him. When Hitler fired him and even threatened to have him shot he had lost his self-control and collapsed. A little later Hitler's pilot Hans Baur saw Morell sitting on his bed, crying like a little child.

Baur, who had been friends with Morell for many years, flew him from Gatow airport to Munich, after which Morell went to Bad Reichenhall in the Bavarian Alps. When he heard of Hitler's suicide, he could not believe it and it wasn't long before Morell ended up in a hospital in the Bavarian village of Gmain. He was physically ill but his mental condition was worsening too. On 21 May, an American journalist found him at the hospital. She described him as a frightened, broken man who had great difficulty speaking about his forced discharge.[26]

Hitler's Minutes

The stenographers from the Führerbunker, Kurt Haagen and Gerhard Herrgesell, also fled to the south. After the dramatic 22 April meeting in which Hitler admitted defeat, Herrgesell was given permission to leave the city to secure the valuable encrypted notes of Hitler's meetings. But his colleague Haagen was told to stay. However, in order to decipher the minutes, a second stenographer was needed and Haagen wanted to leave too. When the men talked about it with their superior, he also got permission to go and that same night both men took a plane to Munich. With them on the plane were more than 100,000 pages of minutes of Hitler's military talks from the period from late 1942 until March 1945.

The papers were taken from the airport to a tunnel on the Obersalzberg were they were hidden. After their work was done, Haagen and Herrgesell took leave somewhere in the Berchtesgadener Land. They couldn't enjoy it for very long, though, because soon the head of the Stenographical Service ordered them to take the minutes from the tunnel to the Hintersee area, where they had to be burned.

One of the exits of the tunnel system on the Obersalzberg.

Herrgesell and Haagen saw to it that the papers were destroyed, but when the Americans entered the region and interrogated Herrgesell, he confessed the minutes were burned near Hintersee. The Americans then took him and one of his colleagues to the location where the minutes were set fire to, to find out that most of the papers had gone up in flames. However, it was possible to save about 1,500 pages that were reasonably intact.[27]

Theodor Gilbert Morell (1886–1948)

On 17 July, the US army reported that they had captured Hitler's private physician Theodor Morell. He successively ended up in five different camps, almost always at the camp's hospital. Morell was constantly questioned about his role and about Hitler's last days. In April 1947, after a heart attack, he ended up in a hospital. The last camp he stayed at was the infamous Dachau Concentration Camp near Munich. On 26 September 1947 he was released. At his own request he was taken to a hospital in Tegernsee where he died on 26 May 1948.

The ditch and the barbed wire fence surrounding Dachau Concentration Camp.

Kurt Haagen (1904(?)–1973)

His early membership of the NSDAP ensured that stenographer Kurt Haagen ended up in an internment camp. But since most stenographers were classed as so-called 'followers', he was released as early as 1946. He began teaching in Cologne and Bonn and became head of the Stenographic Service for the Landtag in North Rhine-Westphalia.

Gerhard Herrgesell (1910–2003)

After Berchtesgaden was taken by the Americans, Hitler's stenographer Gerhard Herrgesell, like some of his colleagues, was no longer allowed to leave Berchtesgaden. He was not locked up, and together with the others, he could walk around the village freely. They were soon instructed to decipher the reclaimed unburnt minutes, but when the work was done, Herrgesell was transferred to an internment camp. He was interrogated a few times in the follow-up trials of Nuremberg. The reason why he was interrogated was his friendship with Rudolf Brandt, Himmler's personal assistant, who was sentenced to death during the Nuremberg trials. Herrgesell was released in April 1948. Three years later he was working as a parliamentary stenographer again.

Robert Ley (1890–1945)

Leader of the state trade union, Robert Ley left Hitler on 21 April. Ley was known for his luxurious lifestyle at state expense and for his addictions to women and alcohol. He abused and mistreated slave labourers.

Ley thought he could lead the resistance from Tyrol after the war. He called himself 'Dr Ernst Distelmeyer' to prevent the Americans from finding him. But on about 15 May he was arrested by American paratroopers at the house of a cobbler in the Bavarian town of Schleching. Ley had not shaved for four days, had lost 30 kilos and was walking around in pyjamas. He told the Americans that on the day Germany capitulated he had been in Linz visiting his children. After that, he said, he didn't care anymore whether he would be arrested or not. He had at least seen his children again.

Ley was taken to the prison camp at Mondorf-les-Bains in Luxembourg and after that he went to the prison behind the Nuremberg Palace of Justice. Ley didn't think of himself as a criminal, but the tribunal thought otherwise. He was held responsible for the abuse of slave labourers and was sentenced to death.

On the night of 25 October, he sat on the toilet bowl of his cell with a piece of cloth in his mouth to muffle any noise he might make. He had a noose around his neck made of strips of towel, which he had attached to the toilet pipe. Leaning forward he strangled himself. In his cell a note was found, that said:

> I wish you all the best! I can no longer bear this shame. Psychologically, I'm fine. The food is good. It's warm in my cell. The Americans behave correctly and are sometimes even friendly. I have enough reading material and I can write whatever I want. I get paper and pencils. They do more than necessary for my health; I am allowed to smoke and I get tobacco and coffee. I am allowed to walk for 20 minutes every day. So far, everything is fine, except for the fact that I am a criminal … and I can't bear that.[28]

Chapter 4

The Escape to the North

Besides Bavaria there was another area still in German hands during the last days of Hitler's life. It was the north-western part of the country between Hamburg, the Danish border and Berlin. Because the Americans and British came from the west, many citizens tried to get to this side of the country, afraid as they were of the Red Army.

On 20 April there were still several German army headquarters and airfields on the north and west side of Berlin but these headquarters were constantly moved towards the north-west corridor to Denmark, following the retreating headquarters of Karl Dönitz.

Dönitz eventually ended up in Flensburg, near the Danish border, and many ministers and important party members tried to get there too. It was their only way out of a hopeless situation.

Hitler's Last Armies

At the end of the war, head of the Supreme Command Wilhelm Keitel and Chief of Operations Alfred Jodl worked from a villa on the west side of Berlin. Their staff had already left for the bunkers of Zossen, south of the city, where the rest of the army organization was located. On 20 April Jodl and Keitel went to the afternoon military meeting at the Führerbunker. Keitel was convinced that Hitler and the Supreme Command had to leave for the south as soon as possible, because the Soviet army was closing in fast. Preparations had already been made and Jodl and Keitel had sent their wives to the Berchtesgadener Land too, where each of them owned a house. A plane was constantly ready for take-off, but Hitler, as discussed above, made clear that he had no plans to leave.[1]

On 22 April, Keitel and Jodl were back at the bunker. Hitler's mood, as mentioned previously, was considerably worse than the day before. He still didn't want to go south, but he ordered Keitel to go there to coordinate the troops. Keitel thought that was a bad idea because soon Hitler would not be able to lead the army from his Berlin bunker. He was afraid that when he left for Bavaria this would lead to a disaster in the north. Therefore, Keitel politely refused to go.[2] Instead he suggested he could go to General Wenck to order him to march to Berlin, together with his Ninth Army. Hitler seemed in agreement.

The supreme command of the German army was still based in this building in Berlin at the time of Hitler's last birthday.

Keitel and Jodl than decided that the Supreme Command of the Army would not stay in Berlin. If Hitler, for whatever reason, could not be reached anymore, they wanted the army's headquarters to be at a location from where they could still make a difference.[3] Keitel then ordered his staff to move from Zossen to Berchtesgaden. Keitel and Jodl would remain in the northern parts of Germany. Their northern armies would be led from the barracks of Krampnitz, near Potsdam.[4]

Jodl immediately went to Potsdam, while Keitel left the city to search for Wenck. From the Reich Chancellery he directly went to Nauen, on the west side of Berlin, but Wenck was difficult to locate. Keitel eventually found him at a forester's house south-west of Berlin. He explained to Wenck that Hitler's fate was in his hands and that he and his troops had to join the Ninth Army to march to Berlin as soon as possible.[5]

A day later, Keitel arrived in Krampnitz, where he slept for just an hour before he had to report back to the Führerbunker. Jodl went with him. After Keitel

Keitel found General Wenck in this forester's house, which has now been converted into a hotel.

The decor in the hotel's dining room still conveys the property's previous purpose.

According to a Neuroofen resident, this building was the most modern in the hamlet after the war because of the facilities put in by the SS.

The cross commemorating the 80,000 soldiers who fell during Wenck's final battle.

had shown Hitler Wenck's written order to move his troops, the news came that Wenck's troops were actually advancing towards Potsdam. Hitler repeated that he would stay in Berlin because he thought the front would collapse if he left the city. Keitel then said that he would visit Wenck again to order the relief of Berlin. After Keitel had spoken with Hitler in private, he and Jodl left the bunker. They would never see Hitler again.[6]

At Krampnitz, officers were already preparing for the next move of the headquarters. The situation was so tense that a commander had panicked when he heard the Soviet Army was nearby. He had blown up an ammunition depot meant for the defence of Berlin, without having received any order to do so. Jodl evacuated the headquarters that night and left with the staff for Neuroofen, a location that had once been developed for Himmler's SS, but had never actually been used.

In the meantime, Keitel had gone to Wenck one more time. Wenck had moved north and put up his headquarters in yet another forester's house. Keitel gave him the order he had taken from the bunker. Wenck then sent all his troops in the direction of Berlin, no matter how pointless that was. Keitel travelled to Neuroofen.[7]

Himmler's Negotiations

Reichsführer of the SS Heinrich Himmler had come from his headquarters at the hospital and convalescent home Hohenlychen to congratulate Hitler on his last birthday. He didn't stay very long in Berlin because he had another appointment that day that was more interesting for him. For a man responsible for the German concentration and extermination camps he had a remarkable encounter at the house of his masseur and personal physician Felix Kersten.[8] There he met with Norbert Masur, a delegate of the World Jewish Congress. Himmler had told Kersten that he was interested in meeting Masur and he offered Masur the release of a group of Jewish women hoping that it would help to reach an agreement with the Western Allies.[9] Masur finalised the deal and secured the release of 7,000 from the concentration camp at Ravensbrück.

Although Hitler didn't want to negotiate with any of his enemies, Himmler did. He had previously spoken about it with the Swedish diplomat Folke Bernadotte and on the night of 23/24 April he had arranged another meeting with him. Himmler met Bernadotte at the Swedish consulate in Lübeck.[10] He asked him if he could arrange a conversation with Eisenhower about a one-sided German surrender on the Western Front. Bernadotte agreed to get in contact with the Western Allies. In the meantime, Himmler had to wait for an answer.

The Hohenlychen sanatorium, used as a headquarters by Himmler.

Himmler met with Norbert Masur, a delegate of the World Jewish Congress, inside this now abandoned villa. It looks like someone continued to live here after the war.

The secluded and dilapidated forest villa where Himmler met Masur.

The reaction to Himmler's peace proposal was predictable – there wasn't going to be any sort of negotiation. But because the BBC deliberately made the information about Himmler's attempt public, word of his actions reached Hitler and Bormann.[11] And they were looking for revenge.

Dönitz's Headquarters

Admiral Karl Dönitz's headquarters Koralle were also still located north of Berlin around the time of Hitler's birthday. But Dönitz was in a hurry, too. He had to go to the Führerbunker to congratulate Hitler and to attend the military meeting there but after that he had to go back to his headquarters as soon as possible. There, his men were already preparing to leave, because the Soviet army was approaching. Two days later his office had moved to the Stadtheide barracks near Plön, north-east of Hamburg. He called his new headquarters Forelle.

Many of the ministers who left Berlin in the second half of April found a place to stay in the vicinity.[12] So did Himmler, although Admiral Dönitz preferred not to have him around. He was fearful of the fact that Himmler was still the leader of the SS which made him a force to be reckoned with. Added to that, Himmler still saw himself as a possible successor of Hitler. When Dönitz met him at some police barracks in Lübeck, Himmler asked the admiral if he would like to serve

In the middle of a forest north of Berlin lie the remains of the gigantic bunkers of Lager Koralle.

On a peninsula near Plön, Dönitz established another headquarters on his way north, called Forelle. There is little to be seen of it today. (*Lenna de Boer*)

This bunker is located near where Dönitz and Himmler met in Lübeck.

him, should the country's leadership fall into his hands. Dönitz gave a vague and evasive answer.[13] But despite Dönitz's cautious rejection, the two men separated on good terms.[14] Himmler remained close to the admiral's headquarters and followed Dönitz when his headquarters moved again.

Hitler and Bormann's Revenge

On 27 April Dönitz visited Keitel and Jodl to discuss the military situation. Keitel was still convinced Hitler had to leave Berlin, and if not, that the Supreme Command had to be split in two definitively. One part had to stay with Dönitz in the north and the other had to go to Kesselring in the south. But when he informed

So as not to be spotted from the air, Keitel and Jodl moved through the forest to their next location. The tracks and roads they took are still in poor condition.

Hitler of his plan, the Führer resolutely rejected it. He wanted to lead the army himself, as long as he was alive.[15]

It was 29 April when Keitel and Jodl took their staff to Himmler's old headquarters in Dobbin, because the Soviet army was closing in again. To go there, they took a detour through the woods near Rheinsberg, so they couldn't be seen by enemy planes. In Dobbin they met Himmler who indicated that he wanted to leave the location the next day. The wireless communication in Dobbin still functioned, and that made it possible for Keitel and Jodl to receive five often quoted questions from Hitler about the current situation at the front. It was the day before Hitler's suicide and Keitel's answers were very clear – the situation was completely hopeless.[16]

Meanwhile, von Greim and Reitsch had arrived at Dönitz's headquarters near Plön. They had left the Führerbunker on 28 April just before midnight with the order to arrest Himmler. They handed it over to Dönitz, so Dönitz now had to deal with Himmler. But Himmler still had his SS and Dönitz wondered why he should act against him now the war seemed almost at an end. He decided to ignore the order even when Bormann repeated it on 30 April. Nevertheless, he had an officer call Himmler to ask him to come to Plön. Himmler, as head of the secret police, must have known that there was some kind of problem because at first he refused to take the telephone. Dönitz was not on the line himself and it was only when Dönitz took the receiver from his officer that Himmler came on the line to listen to what Dönitz had to say. He then promised he would come to Plön.

'A Heroic Death'

On 1 May after Dönitz was informed of Hitler's death a Hamburg radio station brought the news, 'From the Führer's headquarters it is reported that our Führer, Adolf Hitler, fell for Germany this afternoon at his command post at the Reich Chancellery, fighting against Bolshevism to his last breath.'[17] Dönitz also said a few words and spoke of a 'heroic death in the capital of the German Empire'.

Himmler arrived in the middle of the night. He had life insurance with him in the form of a column of armed men and six bodyguards, but Dönitz had no intention of arresting him, he said, after the war. It would have been a tough job if he had tried to do so. When Himmler was inside his office, Dönitz told him that he and not Himmler had been appointed as Hitler's successor. Himmler offered him his services and suggested he could help negotiating with General Eisenhower and Field Marshal Bernard Montgomery, but Dönitz rejected this. Maybe he understood that no Englishman or American would consider negotiating with Himmler.[18] Himmler was not fired yet, but there was nothing more for him to do but stay near Dönitz's command post.

Keitel and Jodl learnt of Hitler's death in these barracks in Neustadt.

In the early morning of that that same day, Keitel and Jodl had been on their way to yet another new temporary office. They encountered rows of refugees and army wagons on their way and they were shot at twice by British planes, but they still knew nothing of Hitler's suicide. After a stay in some barracks in Wismar, they took off for Neustadt. The navy barracks there provided enough space to work at and in addition there was a radio system there that still worked.

In Neustadt Keitel and Jodl finally heard of Hitler's death, after which they had to report to Dönitz as soon as possible. From their newest headquarters it was an hour's drive to Plön. When they got there, Dönitz told them he thought the war should be ended as soon as possible. But first, he said, the evacuation of troops from East Prussia had to be arranged.

A New Cabinet

Now Dönitz was in charge, he had to put together a new cabinet, but although he knew he had to lead the country, he didn't know anything about Hitler's will and the names of the future ministers mentioned in it. In addition, for a while he didn't know exactly what had happened to key figures like Goebbels and Martin Bormann.[19] What he did know was that he did not want to work with Himmler and von Ribbentrop. Perhaps he could have joined forces with the Minister of Education and Science Bernard Rust, who was located nearby.[20] But after being rescued from a suicide attempt, Rust ended up on a psychiatric ward. He subsequently fled on 8 May, the day Germany capitulated, and was successful in his next suicide attempt.

More ministers and well-known national socialists arrived in the vicinity of Plön, such as Minister of Economic Affairs Walter Funk and State Post Minister Wilhelm Ohnesorge. Furthermore, the head of the Chancellery Hans Lammers and Minister of Health Leonardo Conti arrived. Dönitz didn't want them either and he let them know that they were wise to surrender to the Allied Forces.[21]

When Minister of State of the Occupied Territories Alfred Rosenberg turned up at the headquarters, Dönitz said he wanted to get rid of him immediately. Rosenberg was completely drunk and because he had a sprained ankle he was taken to the military hospital at Mürwik, near Flensburg. There he rustled up a medical certificate stating that he was suffering from 'severe bleeding' as a result of his torn ligaments, which prevented him from getting out of bed. Despite this, the British arrested him on 18 May and took him away.[22]

A 'Non-Political' Cabinet

Historian Ian Kershaw rejects the idea that Dönitz – by appointing alternative people to those mentioned by Hitler in his will – had wanted to break with Hitler's policy. It was sometimes assumed that Dönitz had wanted to put together a non-political cabinet, but nothing could be further from the truth, Kershaw said. One of the new cabinet members had participated in the infamous Wannsee Conference, another had contributed to the policy of starvation in Soviet areas and a third member of Dönitz's cabinet had led an Einsatzgruppe responsible for the murder of many Jews.[23] Besides that, Dönitz left the NSDAP and the organization of the Wehrmacht intact.[24]

Like he had told Keitel and Jodl, Dönitz did want the war to end but he found it necessary to postpone the final surrender, so soldiers who had fought in the East and civilians who lived there had more time to get to the West.[25] From the beginning of May Dönitz therefore tried to negotiate with the leaders of the Western armies while he continued to fight in the East.[26] But he had no real control over the situation. He could only order that negotiations should take place in the West 'at the level of army groups', because the Western and Eastern allies still jointly demanded the unconditional surrender of the Germans on both fronts. But if Dönitz complied with this ultimatum it would mean leaving his army and his people in the East out in the cold.[27]

In this villa near Berlin-Wannsee, Nazi officials discussed the final solution to the self-created 'Jewish question'.

Nobody Said One Word

Keitel and Jodl reported back to Dönitz at the beginning of May, while Dönitz had already given the order for his next departure to Mürwik. There Dönitz and his staff used a naval school and the passenger ship *Patria* as office space. Keitel and Jodl decided to go with him to the new headquarters near the Danish border. They took rooms in the barracks near Dönitz and their staff joined them too. The Supreme Command's final strategy became one of letting the army carefully collapse, but with as much delay as possible. Negotiations about the surrender of Germany therefore had to be held with the Allies in the West. Dönitz chose to send Jodl to their headquarters in Reims, France. Jodl would still try to conduct partial negotiations there, but if the other party wouldn't agree, he was also permitted to capitulate completely. The only thing he was required to do before he signed for a complete surrender was to inform Dönitz.[28]

Dönitz moved his headquarters further and further north, but not beyond this property in Flensburg on the Danish border. (*Lenna de Boer*)

Flensburg harbour, near the naval school, where the ship *Patria* was used as an office.

On 6 May, Jodl flew to Reims. Commander-in-Chief Dwight Eisenhower talked to him briefly, but the man knew no mercy. He would only accept Germany's complete surrender and did not for a second consider the fate of the German army in the East. Jodl thus had to consult Dönitz. If Jodl signed, he explained, the hostilities would stop on 9 May, which at least gave the troops in the East a little more time to leave for the West.[29] When Dönitz agreed, Jodl signed the prepared document of surrender on 7 May. After doing so, he tried to speak a few words and asked the victors to be merciful with the German people who had suffered so much. When he had stopped talking, there was silence for a while. None of the representatives of the Allied forces in the room said one word in response.[30]

Complete Capitulation

Keitel had to go to Berlin on 8 May to present the signed papers to the Soviets. He was taken to Stendal in a British plane, and from there the American, British and German representatives flew to Berlin's Tempelhof airport in separate planes.

In Berlin, the American and British men were welcomed by a Russian guard of honour, while Keitel was forced to wait in his plane. When the guard of honour had

The building where the surrender of the German army in Berlin was signed. It is now a museum.

The room where the agreement was signed still looks as it did at the end of the war.

The original City Castle in Berlin was a ruin after the war. It was replaced by the GDR parliament building, but the castle has since been rebuilt.

departed, the Germans were allowed to disembark and were taken to a small villa near the buildings of a technical school. But Keitel had a long wait before meeting the Soviet General Chuikov. Just before midnight he was taken to the building where Chuikov was staying and where the capitulation would be signed. When it was finally over, Keitel was only brought back to Tempelhof after much fuss about whether or not he was allowed to leave. When he was eventually given permission, Keitel once more got to see the ruins of Berlin, driving past the city hall and the imperial palace to Unter den Linden and the Friedrichstraße on his way back to the airport.[31]

Himmler's Escape

It is not sure if Himmler moved with Dönitz from Plön to the area of Flensburg, but he did receive an official written resignation from Dönitz on 6 May.[32] Himmler must have finally understood that there was no room for him in the new Flensburg government. He therefore decided to leave together with a group of SS men, including Hitler's old doctor Karl Brandt, travelling with false documents in the name of 'Heinrich Hizinger'. Himmler was wearing a uniform without badges and an eye patch and he had shaved off his moustache. He was probably headed for

The River Elbe, near the town of Marne, where Himmler and his men crossed in a fishing boat.

During his attempted escape, Himmler stayed at this farm near Bremervörde for several days.

On this island in the middle of the River Oste, a large number of the group with which Himmler was fleeing was arrested.

Bavaria.[33] As long as they were in the north, they had the advantage they hardly stood out among all the other German soldiers roaming about.

An article published in the British magazine *After the Battle* in the 1970s describes Himmler's flight from 10 May.[34] On that day Himmler and his group left the headquarters in Flensburg, it says. Two days later the group arrived in separate cars at the abandoned village of Marne on the Elbe. There, the men left their cars behind and walked to the wide mouth of the Elbe. For a small fee a fisherman took them to the other side, sailing them up the smaller River Oste to the village of Neuhaus. On that side of the Elbe the British had control over Schleswig-Holstein.

On 18 May Himmler and his men arrived at Bremervörde, where they moved into a farm at the local Waldstraße for the time being. On the other side of the village was a double bridge crossing the River Oste and an island in the middle. Of the two bridges the eastern one had been blown up and replaced with a temporary structure. The other bridge was damaged but could still be used. One of the men went to take a look at the bridge that could be crossed, while the others stayed at the farm. On the island was a pumping station with a mill where British soldiers had set up their headquarters. The bridge was therefore guarded by British soldiers, who in particular checked German soldiers who wished to get to the other side of the river.

On the afternoon of 20 May two of the men from Himmler's group went to take another look. They agreed that they would come back to pick up the others when it was safe enough to cross the bridge. Both men got in line at the checkpoint, where members of the Allied intelligence were checking for war criminals. They took the men in, seemingly because they looked suspicious to them, and brought them to their headquarters inside the mill. During interrogation one of the men, a doctor, said that he had a number of sick people under his care with whom he wanted to cross the bridge. The British officers found this quite remarkable but they pretended that they believed this story and offered the men two trucks to transport the other men to the bridge. When the doctor came back with the other men that were still at the farm, the British interrogated the other Germans too. It didn't take very long for them to discover the doctor's story did not match the account given by the others, and at about 1800 hours the Germans were arrested and taken to a soldiers' camp in Westertimke.

But Himmler and two of his companions had not been with the group when the trucks arrived at the bridge. The reason for this is unknown, but several members of the group told the British interrogators that there were three men missing. The British kept an eye out for the three men, but it wasn't until 22 May that they spotted Himmler and his companions in the main street of Bremervörde, walking in the direction of the bridge. They didn't know that the infamous Heinrich

Himmler was one of them, but the men behaved so inconspicuously that it became noticeable. They were arrested before they even arrived at the bridge and Himmler and his men were also detained inside the mill on the little island in the river. They spent the night there and still none of the British realized who they had arrested.

The next day Himmler and his escorts were taken to the same camp in Westertimke as the other men, after a stopover in Zeven where the arrest had to be reported. Himmler was then taken through Fallingbostel to the Civil Interrogation Camp at Kolkhagen, west of Barnstedt.

A Second Version of the Story

There is a second story about Himmler's flight. This also starts off with Himmler being on the run under his new name 'Heinrich Hizinger', together with two of his adjutants. But their arrest took place at a different location, according to this other account.[35] Reports state that Soviet soldiers, who had been on patrol with British soldiers, arrested them about 4 miles from Bremervörde.[36] The combination of British and Russian soldiers working together was not as strange as it seems today. At the nearby Sanbostel Camp Russian and Polish prisoners of war had been incarcerated during the Third Reich. Following their liberation by the Western troops some of them then helped the British army.

Sanbostel held Russian and Polish soldiers who collaborated with the British at the end of the war.

The outskirts of the village of Minstedt, where Russian soldiers claimed that they arrested Himmler.

According to the soldiers it was 21 May when the British patrol, together with two Soviet soldiers, were moving around Minstedt. When the British took a coffee break at 1900 hours, the Soviets did an extra round. During that round they saw three German men coming out of the trees somewhere along the edge of the small village. The soldiers shouted to them to stop, but the Germans tried to escape. After the Soviets gave a warning shot, the Germans had no choice but to stand still. The Soviets took them to the British post immediately, where the decision was made to transport them to the camp at Seedorf, about 6 miles away.[37] From there they were taken to Bremervörde, where they were detained for two days.[38]

After that, both versions of Himmler's flight come together at the same location and on the same date: the camp at Kolkhagen, near Barnstedt, on 23 May. As soon as Himmler entered that camp, it is said that he was recognized by the Gauleiter of Hamburg, who was also imprisoned there. Knowledge of his recognition would have been a risk for Himmler and maybe that's the reason why he asked to talk to the camp's commander. When Himmler and his company entered the commander's room, the man in charge found them to be such a peculiar trio that he had them taken into custody, although he had no proof of them having done anything wrong. The commander ordered no one to speak to them without him knowing about it. Realizing it was over, Himmler took off his eye patch and put on his familiar glasses. With a soft voice he introduced himself as Heinrich Himmler.[39]

Himmler's Death

Himmler was searched thoroughly at Kolkhagen. A small, hollow copper tube was found in his belongings, which presumably had contained a suicide capsule. When asked what it was, Himmler answered that it was used for administering medicine to treat abdominal pain. The officers had no choice but to order Himmler to undress and conduct a complete body search. Fearing the possibility that Himmler was holding a capsule of cyanide in his mouth, this part of his body was not examined. Instead, bread and tea were brought to Himmler, who ate and drank quietly while being closely observed.[40] Nothing untoward happened and Himmler was picked up by soldiers from the headquarters at Lüneburg. It was 2330 hours when they took him there and as soon as he arrived he had to undergo another full body search again. At the end of it the doctor who carried out the examination asked Himmler to open his mouth and when Himmler did so the doctor saw something inside his mouth that did not belong there. He immediately stuck his finger between

Himmler committed suicide in a room on the left-hand side of this house.

In the corner room on the ground floor, Himmler bit through a cyanide capsule.

One of the locations where Himmler is said to have been buried is a forest near Lüneburg.

his teeth, but Himmler closed his jaws even quicker and bit through the cyanide capsule he had concealed there.[41] The men inside the office immediately tried to flush away the poison with water, but this had little effect. Himmler died on the floor of a room in a house in Lüneburg on 23 May 1945.[42]

Three days later, the body of Heinrich Himmler, one of the greatest war criminals of the Third Reich, was buried. It is not known where, but some say it was in Lüneburg.[43] Others suggest it was in the Lüneburger Heide and a forest near Lüneburg.[44] The exact location remains undetermined, and the British soldiers who knew kept their mouths shut for the rest of their lives.

Von Ribbentrop's Final Days

Foreign Minister Joachim von Ribbentrop tried to join Dönitz in Flensburg too, but on 20 April 1945 he was still some distance away. To congratulate Hitler, he only had to cross the street from his so-called Dienststelle Ribbentrop on Wilhelmstraße to get to the Reich Chancellery. His office building, formerly used by Rudolf Heß and Martin Bormann, had few staff left. He barely needed his staff anymore and on 13 April he had sent most of them to his summer residence, Fuschl Castle, in Austria. Since Hitler wanted to continue fighting until the end, negotiations with foreign powers were out of the question. But Hitler had lost interest in the minister and his work much earlier and von Ribbentrop must have been aware of that.

Rudolf Heß, Martin Bormann and Joachim von Ribbentrop successively had their offices in this building on Wilhelmstraße. The head of the Hitler Youth, Arthur Axmann, was also to follow.

Göring's first message requesting a sign of life from Hitler was followed by a second telegram addressed to von Ribbentrop. With that message he probably thought he could earn back some respect from the Führer. As soon as it arrived, von Ribbentrop crossed the street and brought the telegram to the bunker. With that, he proved he was still loyal to Hitler.

As discussed above, Göring wrote that he wanted von Ribbentrop to come to Berchtesgaden if Hitler didn't give a sign of life, and Bormann and Hitler took this as the absolute proof Göring was forging a plot against Hitler. He was even trying to involve von Ribbentrop in his attempt to seize power, they must have thought.

As a reward for this demonstration of loyalty von Ribbentrop was allowed to visit Hitler once more, even though Hitler did not feel like seeing him at all. He used the meeting to get rid of him and ordered the faithful minister to leave Berlin to negotiate with the British one more time.[45]

Von Ribbentrop's Regret

The next day von Ribbentrop left Berlin, but he was barely out of the city before he regretted the decision. Maybe he started doubting his chances and he might have realized that he had not received a specific plan from Hitler about how to get in contact with the key British politicians or army leaders. He was still in the nearby town of Nauen when he stopped the car and tried to get in contact with Hitler's bunker. When someone answered the telephone he asked if they could send a plane to pick him up and bring him back to Berlin, but Hitler didn't want to see him anymore.

Now von Ribbentrop only had one way to go – Dönitz's headquarters. On Hitler's dying day, he arrived by plane at the military airfield of Wittstock.[46] He finally reached Plön at the beginning of May and found himself a place near Dönitz's headquarters. Dönitz later said that he had no intention of using him and that he

The corner of Lentzeallee in Berlin. This is where the sloping plot of Ribbentrop's villa began. The house no longer exists.

thought von Ribbentrop was too stupid to dance for the Devil.[47] He appointed former Minister of Finance under Hitler Count Johann Ludwig Schwerin von Krosigk as his successor. For von Ribbentrop this meant that he had to stay behind when Dönitz moved to Flensburg.[48]

'Johann Riese' Travels to Hamburg

Von Ribbentrop then decided to go to Hamburg, which had already fallen into British hands. Little was left of the city, but at least the war was over by the time he got there. While the local people emerged from their cellars and ruined houses, von Ribbentrop went into hiding.[49] Through a wine merchant he knew, he met a woman in one of the suburbs who rented rooms. He took a room on the fifth floor, adopted the name 'Johann Riese' and stayed inside the house as much as he could. He only went out smartly dressed, with sunglasses on and wearing a

The site of Ribbentrop's betrayal. The British Security Headquarters was located here. It is now the building of the US Consulate General.

black diplomat's hat.[50] But he had nothing more to do in Hamburg than to wait for what was to come. Maybe that's the reason he started writing letters to British politicians in which he pointed out that Hitler had wanted nothing but peace with Great Britain and that he himself did not understand the British hatred towards the Germans.[51] Of course, there was no longer any point in negotiating, but with the letters he wrote, he at least fulfilled the assignment he said he had received from Hitler. But it was also a self-justification. After all, von Ribbentrop had been the Minister of Foreign Affairs during the war with Great Britain.

After a while, when many of the prominent national socialists who were still alive had already surrendered or been arrested, von Ribbentrop remained free and after the arrest of the Dönitz cabinet he was actively hunted down. This came to an end on 14 June when the son of the wine merchant who had helped von Ribbentrop find a room went to the British Headquarters for Security in Hamburg to inform them of his whereabouts. One Belgian and three British security officers went to pick him up and found him sleeping in his room.[52]

Von Ribbentrop told his psychiatrist Leon Goldensohn, who he met during his time at the Nuremberg trials, that he had planned to commit suicide, and that he had always carried his cyanide capsule with him. But when the British officers arrested him and searched him, he handed them the poison himself.[53]

The officers immediately informed Colonel Niall MacDermot about finding von Ribbentrop. The colonel was very surprised about the arrest because he had just learned that the Americans had arrested von Ribbentrop in Bremen.

But coincidentally von Ribbentrop's sister had arrived at the port of Hamburg by ship. She was taken to her brother, and she could confirm that he was the real von Ribbentrop.[54] When he was searched he was found to be in possession of three letters: one for Vincent Churchill, one for Field Marshal Montgomery and one for Foreign Minister Anthony Eden. Even though he had never sent the letters, they were passed on to the addressees.[55] There was one exception – one of the letters was sent to a certain Winston Churchill instead of the mysterious Vincent . . .

Doubting Albert Speer

Minister of Armaments Albert Speer was thinking of the future after his first departure from the Führerbunker. Speer travelled from Berlin to Altranft, north-east of the city.[56] Historian Joachim Fest, who worked a good deal with Speer after the war, did not mention this stopover in his biography of Speer, but vaguely suggested that he went to his family on an estate in Schleswig-Holstein and that he left for Hamburg a day later.[57]

In recent Speer biographies, such as the one by Magnus Brechtken, Speer is described as taking another route. According to Brechtken, Speer did not go

In his bid to transform Berlin into the grandiose city of Germania, Albert Speer moved this victory column from the square in front of the Reichstag to a roundabout in the middle of Tiergarten park.

directly to the north-western part of the country at all, but in the opposite direction to the north-east, as Speer once confessed after the war. He took a strange route towards the east where the Red Army came from, but Speer pretended it was just an aimless trip without any significance. Brechtken raised the question why Speer made such a pointless trip, taking such a big risk instead of heading for Hamburg. Speer said it wasn't that dangerous – only a few Soviet planes passed by and when he heard that the Red Army was in the area, he quickly turned around.

Or was it Speer's Altranft estate that was so important to him that he risked his life for it? Speer had planned a luxurious villa for himself there, but it was never finished, although Brechtken pointed out that it is possible there were still some papers, valuables or important items stored at the estate that he wanted to secure.[58] Speer was never very clear about it.

Meeting Hitler One More Time

After his detour Speer drove past Berlin on the north side and travelled to Hamburg. Together with his adjutant Manfred von Poser, he is said to have prevented some naval bridges and other important parts of the harbour from being blown up, but to what extent this statement was a part of Speer's self-defence tactics, is difficult to say.[59]

Speer's castle in Sigrön, which still contained valuables that he wanted to secure at the end of the war.

After reaching Hamburg he went back to Berlin within a day. It was 22 April and once again he made a detour, this time past his Sigrön estate, near Bad Wilsnack.[60] Fest later claimed he did not do this.[61] But Speer had had a castle in Sigrön for a long time and it is possible he had stored some valuable things there too. He now had them taken elsewhere, after which he set off for Berlin. He got stranded about 25 miles from the city, he said. As he couldn't get through, he decided to drive to Rechlin instead to catch a plane that took him to Gatow. From there he had planned to fly to the centre of Berlin. Because Speer wasn't clear about this route either, Brechtken suspected there might have been something interesting for him to do on that part of the route as well. What it was is unknown. The only thing that is known is that Speer arrived at the Führerbunker on 23 April.[62]

Speer and Dönitz

After he had seen Hitler for the last time, Speer flew back to Rechlin, after which he took some time to visit Himmler at Hohenlychen.[63] He preferred to talk as little as possible about his meeting with the SS leader after the war, which might explain why he didn't give many details about his detour through Rechlin.[64] After the meeting he drove back to the airport and flew to Hamburg, where he stayed at

Albert Speer spent a short time in Hamburg at the Hotel Atlantic before going to Eutin where a train was waiting for him.

Speer did not go to Eutin to board the train, but to check on his valuable belongings that had been put into the train carriages.

the famous Hotel Atlantic. On Wednesday his journey continued to Eutin.[65] Speer spent the night near some of his railway wagons there, at an estate or at the army barracks nearby. His wagons stood on a siding near the Eutiner See and were filled with his possessions and art collection.[66]

In the days that followed, Speer visited his family in Kappeln, about 60 miles from Eutin, but eventually even Speer had to join admiral Dönitz in Plön. When Dönitz moved his headquarters to Flensburg, Speer followed him. At the invitation of an acquaintance, he worked with his adjutants and secretaries in Glücksburg Castle, where he might have encountered Himmler during another mysterious meeting.[67] Unlike Himmler, Speer became part of the Dönitz government as Minister of Economy, Armaments, Ammunition and War Production. On 3 May Speer addressed the German people in a radio broadcast, calling on them to be brave during the difficult times they were going through.[68]

The Arrest of the Flensburg Government

It took until 15 May before the Americans started interrogating Albert Speer at Glücksburg Castle. That did not mean that he was imprisoned immediately. He could still move about freely and was even allowed to drive to see his family in the evenings. These privileges ended on 23 May, when he was arrested with the rest of the Dönitz government. Coincidentally, that took place on the same day Himmler committed suicide. The arrest marked the end of a government that, from the beginning, had not had much to say about the future of Germany.

Keitel had been disposed of before. After he had signed the surrender in Berlin, he had returned to Flensburg, but when an American delegation came to the city he was arrested. The Americans, who took over the luxury ship *Patria*, invited Dönitz aboard the ship on 13 May for a conversation. There the Americans explained to him that they were about to arrest Keitel. Keitel himself was invited half an hour later, so there was no opportunity for the two Germans to speak to each other. An American general told Keitel that he would be taken away as a prisoner of war. His plane would leave within a few hours. He was only allowed to return to his headquarters, where he said goodbye to Dönitz and could pass over some ongoing business to Jodl.

The plane took him to Luxembourg, where he ended up at the Allied Interrogation Centre in the Ashcan Camp in Mondorf-les-Bains. The national commissioner of the Netherlands Arthur Seyss-Inquart was already imprisoned there. Later, all the important leaders of the Third Reich who were still alive were taken there. On 23 May Dönitz and Jodl were summoned to the *Patria* and just like Speer they

From this local airport, Jodl, Dönitz and Speer were flown to Luxembourg where they were imprisoned together with other high-ranking Nazis.

were arrested there too. Jodl was allowed to return to the German headquarters before they left, but British army officers were already inside the building. All the employees were herded together while the offices were searched. Jodl was taken to the police station, where Dönitz and Speer were already being held. The three men were driven to an airfield near Flensburg to be flown to Luxembourg. There they not only met Göring again, but also von Papen, Rosenberg, Keitel, Seyss-Inquart, Ley, Frank, Wilhelm Frick, Funk, Streicher, von Ribbentrop, von Neurath and Schwerin von Krosigk.[69]

Eckhard Christian (1907–85)

Air Force General Eckhard Christian was married to Hitler's secretary Gerda Christian. From 1943 he was present at Hitler's headquarters as one of the representatives of Hermann Göring. After the dramatic meeting on 22 April, Christian left Berlin and worked for a short time as head of the liaison staff of Luftwaffe North. With the stream of fleeing politicians, civil servants and army officials he went to Flensburg, where he was arrested by the British on 5 May 1945. After two years' imprisonment, he was released.

Joachim von Ribbentrop (1893–1946)

On 12 August, von Ribbentrop and a number of other prominent figures were taken by plane to Nuremberg. He ended up in prison at the Palace of Justice. He had few real friends there and fell into a depression in these new surroundings. On 1 October 1946 he was sentenced to death by hanging. On the morning of 16 October, he was taken to the gallows. After his last words, in which he said that he hoped that God would be with Germany and that there would be peace between the East and West, he was hanged. Witnesses said it took at least 10 minutes before he was dead.[70]

Wilhelm Keitel (1882–1946)

In October 1945, Field Marshal Wilhelm Keitel was flown from Luxembourg to Nuremberg, where he was brought before the court. He wrote his memoirs in the prison behind the courthouse. At the end he stated: 'I began my term as prisoner of war on 13th May, 1945 at Mondorf. I was transferred to a prison cell at Nuremberg on the 13th August, and I am waiting for my execution on 13th October, 1946.' The execution took place three days later, on 16 October 1946. Keitel was hanged.

Alfred Jodl (1890–1946)

Head of operations of the Supreme Command, Alfred Jodl also appeared before the judges of Nuremberg. He was sentenced to death there and hanged on 16 October 1946. He was cremated at the Ostfriedhof in Munich. His ashes were scattered in the Wentzbach, a tributary of the River Isar, just like the ashes of Göring and Keitel.

Karl Dönitz (1891–1980)

Admiral Karl Dönitz was tried in Nuremberg after his stay at Ashcan Camp, Mondorf-les-Bains. He was sentenced to ten years in prison for his crimes. He served his time at Spandau Prison in Berlin. After that, he lived in Germany until the end of 1980.

Albert Speer (1905–81)

After Speer left the Allied Interrogation Centre in Ashcan Camp, he spent some time in a camp for technicians in Chesnay, near Paris. After that he was brought back to Germany, where he stayed at the British Dustbin Camp located at the former Göring headquarters of Kransberg Castle, near Bad Nauheim. At the end of September, he was picked up there and taken to Nuremberg through interrogation camp at Oberursel. He was locked up in the prison behind the Palace of Justice where he was to be tried. He was sentenced to twenty years' imprisonment, which he served at Spandau Prison. On 1 October 1966 he was released.

Spandau prison was demolished immediately after the death of the last prisoner, Rudolf Heß. Trees planted by Speer in the prison garden can still be seen at the edge of a car park.

Speer's efforts to minimize any financial worries after the war had paid off. He lived the rest of his life in luxury, but the books he wrote also earned him a lot of money. From his family villa in Heidelberg he published several bestsellers in which he gave his own vision of the history of the Third Reich. Albert Speer died of a stroke in London in 1981, during a visit to his mistress.

Chapter 5

Fleeing Through Berlin's Tiergarten

On 29 April, adjutants von Loringhoven, Boldt and Weiss were waiting along the Hermann-Göring-Straße for the right moment to leave the Chancellery grounds. After they managed to get permission to leave Hitler's bunker, von Loringhoven had brought some food, maps and a machine gun to a bunker on the other side of the plot. They wanted to cross the street diagonally, towards the large city park Tiergarten. But crossing the street was risky and they had to wait for the best moment to go. The Soviet army was nearby and the street was in disarray. Along the bunker wall, which was connected to the Führerbunker through cellar corridors, they waited until a mortar attack had stopped. Then they crawled onto the street, while the bullets of a machine gun were still flying over their heads and the thick black smoke slowly came in from the Potsdamer Platz,

This photograph was taken approximately on the spot where Hitler's adjutants were waiting to cross the street on 29 April. Behind the modern buildings is Tiergarten Park.

The surroundings of Zoo station have changed dramatically since the adjutants took refuge there, but the roof structure of the station still looks like it did in the 1940s.

and went for it. Through craters and alongside the corpses of soldiers and civilians, the adjutants moved to the edge of the park, but their progress was slow even after entering the Tiergarten. The three men had planned to go straight through the park to the west, but it took a great deal of time to reach the zoo on that side of the park. There were craters all over the place and from every corner there was the threat of gunfire. At one point it became so dangerous that the adjutants decided it was better to continue their journey with the protection of the houses on the edge of the park. There they went on, past wrecks of cars, groups of dead people in pits and burning buildings. When they finally reached the other side of the park, they rested for a while in the damaged planetarium and then quickly moved on to a shelter under Zoo station. It was 1800 hours – a 2-mile walk had taken them hours.

Hitler's Will

Earlier that day, three couriers had been sent out too. They had to secure Hitler's will. After it was copied and signed in triplicate at 0400 hours, it had to be taken to three different places. Army deputy Johannmeyer was ordered to bring a copy to General Field Marshal Ferdinand Schörner in Czechoslovakia, deputy Zander had to bring a copy to Dönitz and Chief of Press Heinz Lorenz had to bring the

The couriers carrying Hitler's will went straight into the Tiergarten at this spot. On the right is today's Ebertstraße, which leads past the Holocaust Memorial to the Brandenburg Gate.

original to Munich, where it was to be lodged in the archives. Their dangerous mission started at 0800 hours and a certain Corporal Hummerich accompanied them. These four men also left the grounds of the Reich Chancellery from the bunkers and garages at the rear of the Chancellery grounds and crossed the same road as the adjutants, trying to find the shortest way out through the Tiergarten.

Along Ruined Facades

Air Force Adjutant von Below was the last person to leave the bunker taking almost the same route. Hitler had given him permission to leave on 29 April too and after the last briefing he attended, he took some bread, a submachine gun and an ampoule of cyanide, which he had been allocated previously. Together with his young colleague Heinz Mathiesung, he set off for the Tiergarten. They too had to pick their way through bomb craters, downed cables and the rubble of collapsed houses before they reached the Brandenburg Gate. They chose to follow the street that ran alongside the city park. It had still been in use as a runway for aeroplanes shortly before. Past the Siegessäule, they turned left at the track of an S-Bahn and reached the large above-ground flakturm of the park, that also served as a shelter. Von Below consulted with the commander regarding the route to follow,

Von Below, on his flight out of the city, went past the park to the Brandenburg Gate. There he turned left and walked with his subordinate alongside the park to the west.

The hippopotamus pool at Berlin Zoo is located where the above-ground flakturm bunker once stood.

and especially the whereabouts of the enemy. The man advised them to go to the Olympic Stadium, where he knew another German unit was stationed. There they should ask how to get out of the city.

Moving cautiously in front of the facades of ruined houses on the Kantstraße, near the famous Kurfürstendamm, they edged towards the Adolf-Hitler Platz. Although the stadium was not that far away from where they were, it took a long time to get through the Reichsstraße and enter the stadium grounds. There, one of the officers of the army unit advised them to continue their journey as soon as possible, because he did not know what the next day would bring.

The couriers had already taken a similar route from the park to the stadium. Through the Joachimstraße and along the Kurfürstendamm, they had arrived at the Adolf-Hitler Platz too. But there they were lucky because a lieutenant,

The Olympic Stadium, Berlin. To get to the Havel River, von Below had to pass the stadium, which was being guarded by members of the Hitler Youth.

who was responsible for that part of the city, could arrange a car and a driver to transport them through the districts of Charlottenburg and Halensee to the Olympic Stadium. There they stayed for a few hours in a room on the west side of the building together with a group of Hitler Youth boys. Having rested, the couriers resumed their journey. As they had Hitler's will in their possession they would be a very interesting catch, so they had to be quick and careful at the same time. Through the western part of the city, which was already crawling with Soviet soldiers, they tried to get to the village of Pichelsdorf, near the Havel River.

Sailing the Havel

The bridge over the Havel near Pichelsdorf was also the target for adjutants von Loringhoven, Boldt and Weiss. Together with other men that joined them early in the morning of 30 April, including Colonel von Below, they tried to reach the river there. From the stadium, it was only about 2½ miles to Pichelsdorf, but to get to the peninsula on which the village was situated, they had to cross the bridge. And that was a problem, because although the bridge that was still in German hands, the adjutants could see that from a distance Soviet tanks had their guns aimed at it. After some discussion they decided to take their chances. They ran across the bridge hoping the tanks were not ready to fire until they crossed it. But nothing happened. Chances were that the Soviet soldiers were still asleep.

On the peninsula that lay between two arms of the river, the Germans searched for boats they could use. They wanted to sail to the south and hoped they could still land near the Pfaueninsel on the west bank. From there they would try to travel further on foot. The commander of the battalion of boys that controlled the Pichelsdorf peninsula asked one of his lads to bring von Below, Mathiesung and the

To get to Pichelsdorf the men had to cross two bridges held at gunpoint by Soviet tanks. This is the current Freybrücke, the original bridge having been demolished.

A section of the river near Pichelsdorf.

Rowing on the Havel River was dangerous because there were many Soviet soldiers in the vicinity, especially on the west bank.

The island of Pfaueninsel, as seen from Wannsee Island.

three adjutants to some boats they could use. But as day was dawning, they had to wait for hours before they could leave.

When it finally became dark, they got into the boats and sailed as quietly as they could to the centre of the river where they let the current take them south. After a while they were forced to row towards the west bank due to a blockage in the river. Now they had to operate even more quietly, because the Red Army already controlled the area they were in. They could even hear the voices of Soviet soldiers emanating from the various villas on the bank. It was already 1 May and it took them until 0300 hours to finally pass Schwanenwerder Island, where famous party members such as Goebbels and Speer had owned villas. There the river split. Going to the right would bring them to the Pfaueninsel and going left would bring them to the Wannsee Lake. In between lay the large Wannsee Island which was still in German hands.

Going Ashore

Von Below chose to go directly to the west bank. But the adjutants went ashore on the island. There they soon ran into German troops and they discovered that the couriers had also landed there. The men knew each other from the Führerbunker, but it is not clear if they understood what either one was doing there and they had different missions. That meant that the couriers of Hitler's will were free to go, because they had a special assignment, but the adjutants had left the bunker to join Wenck's troops. Because the German soldiers on the island were about to march in the direction of Potsdam, towards Wenck's army, the three men were trapped. In the bunker they had thought up the nonsensical task of joining Wenck, even though they had never intended to do so. They had used it as an excuse to leave the bunker, but now their assignment was keeping them from going west and they had no choice but to join the departing troops because otherwise they could be suspected of desertion.

Von Below and his colleague had already set course for the west bank where they soon saw the houses of the Military Academy near Gatow. They carefully rowed to the shore, hoping there were no Soviet soldiers waiting for them. But there was no one there. When they had set foot on land, they immediately went in the direction of the Dalgow-Döberitz military area. From there they wanted to walk to the sector of the Western Allies.

The couriers had left Wannsee Island too and went to the Pfaueninsel. There they waited inside a bunker until nightfall. They put on civilian clothes and, at some point, they made radio contact with Dönitz. They still had a real mission and therefore tried to arrange a plane that could take them directly to him. They gave their position and waited for the plane to arrive. But before it came the Soviets took the island under fire, so the men were forced to take their canoes onto the river. When the plane finally came to pick them up, it was fired upon too. Before they could get inside, the plane took off without them. Johannmeyer, Zander and Lorenz had no choice but to head for Potsdam and to try to reach the River Elbe from there. Behind the river was the British sector and if they made it there, they might be able to still deliver the copies of Hitler's will. But when they finally got to the Elbe, it was too late. Germany had surrendered. They decided to hide the will and its copies at three different locations. After that they would try to pick up their former lives again.

A Tube of Pills

On Wannsee Island adjutants von Loringhoven, Boldt and Weiss travelled with the troops they had come across. But as soon as an opportunity arose, they took off into the trees. They waited until the other German soldiers had left and travelled further on their own. At some point Weiss suggested he would take the lead as a scout. The other two had to follow him from a distance. But after a while Weiss had gone. Von Loringhoven and Boldt suspected he had been captured and in fear they hid in a ditch in the woods. In the distance they could hear Soviet soldiers searching the area with dogs.

Laying in a ditch, not knowing what would happen, made Boldt very nervous and after a while he couldn't hold out any longer and made a reckless decision. He

Von Lornighoven and Boldt hid in a ditch in the woods on Wannsee Island.

The bridge over the Teltow Canal. Here von Loringhoven saw his comrade Weiss pass by.

was lucky that von Loringhoven just in time saw that he was about to swallow a complete tube of pills. He intervened and prevented Boldt from swallowing all the pills. Then he made sure his comrade spat out most of the pills he had already swallowed. He took Boldt to a railwaymen's hut, where they hid for two nights. Inside the hut they exchanged their army uniforms for the working clothes they found there. On 3 May they finally tried to get off the island, across the bridge over the Teltow Canal. When they reached the bridge a stream of Soviet soldiers started crossing simultaneously. The Battle of Berlin had already ended and they were wearing civilian clothes, so when one of the Soviet soldiers asked them if they knew the way to Jüterbog, they had a good chance to just leave the island. Von Loringhoven still pretended to be French and said that he did not understand the Russian man. Exactly at that moment von Loringhoven saw their comrade Weiss passing on an army truck full of German prisoners. Weiss didn't see them and, of course, von Loringhoven acted as if he hadn't seen Weiss either.

Almost Safe

The two adjutants agreed that they would pretend to be forced labourers from Luxembourg and, apart from encountering a number of checkpoints, the rest of the journey went reasonably well. Only when von Loringhoven and Boldt arrived near Wittenberg on about 8 May were they taken off the street to a camp housing other foreign workers. They registered under false names and left as soon as possible. They could do this because they were not held as prisoners there. When they finally arrived at the Elbe, they asked a fisherman to bring them to the other side because they weren't allowed to cross the damaged city bridge. When they had crossed the Elbe, they still weren't in the American sector. They had to cross one more river, called the Mulde. On 11 May the men swam across the cold river that was half a mile wide. When they reached the other side they went their separate ways. Boldt went to his family in Lübeck and von Loringhoven went to Leipzig.

Working at the Local Inn

When von Below and Mathiesung arrived on the west side of the Dalgow-Döberitz military area, they rested for a while. As it was crowded with Russians there, they hid in the trees until it was dark. With the help of a compass, they headed north-west and as soon as they got the chance they changed their military uniforms for civilian clothes. They had already seen large groups of civilians trying to escape to the west, and they could have joined them, but they chose to take a different route. That turned out to be a mistake, because when they arrived at a Soviet checkpoint

The military buildings of Dalgow-Döberitz, opposite the Olympic Village outside Berlin. Von Below and Mathiesung hid near here until nightfall.

To get to the river from the village of Sandau, von Below and Mathiesung first had to cross the wide floodplains.

Old buildings in a street in Havelberg.

they were arrested immediately. Apparently, the guards did not trust the two men travelling alone. They were put on a truck with other prisoners, and it seemed this was the end of their attempted escape.

But von Below and Mathiesung were not going to be caught that easy. They managed to jump off when the truck had to slow down passing a group of German refugees and they immediately joined the group. On 3 May they arrived at the village of Friesack, where the road was blocked. They could do nothing but wait until they were able to travel onwards, so they sought a place to stay.

After a night in an empty house, they woke up to discover the blockade had already been lifted. When they came to the village of Sandau they found an empty villa where they stayed for a while. From the house the Elbe was easy to reach and there were still food and drink inside. The only thing that stood between them and the Western Allies was the river and when they had rested and had had enough to eat, they tried to cross it. But they got caught again and this time they were taken to a prison camp. However, it was so poorly guarded that their fellow prisoners, most of whom probably didn't have to worry about being imprisoned for much longer, helped them find a way out.

Because things had almost gone wrong twice now, von Below decided to wait until there was a real chance to cross the river. In the town of Havelberg, a little further down the road, they went to the police to report themselves, as they were supposed to do. They were given shelter in a damaged inn on condition that they helped the old man who owned it to rebuild it. The building had been pretty badly damaged during the war and for about four weeks von Below and Mathiesung were kept busy repairing the entire roof. After that, the circumstances had changed and now it seemed possible to travel through Germany again. This was the moment they had waited for. Von Below and Mathiesung said goodbye to the owner of the inn and went their separate ways.[1]

Rudolf Weiss (1910–58) – Bernd Freytag von Loringhoven (1914–2007) – Gerhard Boldt (1918–81)

The former buildings of Adelheide Camp, near Delmenhorst, are still in use but as a military barracks.

Not much is known about adjutant Rudolf Weiss, who was the first adjutant to be arrested. He disappeared for five years in a prisoner-of-war camp in the Soviet Union, after which he most likely returned to Germany.

As both von Loringhoven and Boldt published a book about their experiences more is known about their fate. Adjutant Bernd Freytag von Loringhoven managed to get very close to his family, but near the Völkerschlachtdenkmal area in Leipzig he was taken off the street by an American soldier who did not believe his story about him being a slave labourer from Luxembourg. After being locked up in a cellar for a few days, he ended up in Camp Helfta, together with 25,000 other German soldiers. Before Christmas a British major took him to the interrogation camp at Bad Nenndorf, near Hanover, which was located in some converted rooms of a public bathhouse. After four weeks he ended up in a camp near Ostend and when he left that, he went to the Munsterlager on the Lüneberger Heide. After a stay in Adelheide Camp, near Delmenhorst, he was released in 1948.

Adjutant Gerhard Boldt reached his family in Lübeck, but was arrested by the British. He ended up in an internment and interrogation camp. In the 1970s there was some controversy about Boldt's book *Hitler's Last Days*. Critics said he had copied the details of what had happened inside the Führerbunker from other sources.

Heinz Lorenz (1913–85) – Wilhelm Zander (1911–74) – Willy Johannmeyer (1915–70)

Chief of Press Heinz Lorenz changed his identity after the capitulation of Germany and adopted the guise of a Luxembourg journalist for a time. In autumn 1945 he ended up in Fallingbostel Camp in the north of Germany. There he revealed to the interrogators who he really was and removed Hitler's original testament with the Goebbels appendix from behind the lining of his jacket, where he had concealed it. He remained in captivity until halfway through 1947. After that he worked for a while as a secretary and stenographer for the German Bundestag.

Martin Bormann's adjutant Wilhelm Zander, who had also taken on a different identity, hid his documents in a suitcase near Lake Tegernsee. When they were found, Hitler's wedding papers were there too. He was arrested in the American zone and imprisoned for some time. After his release he lived in Munich.

Wehrmacht officer Willy Johannmeyer hid his copy of the will in a bottle buried in his family's back garden in Iserlohn, Sauerland. After the war, he worked for various companies, including one based in Frankfurt am Main.

A building at Fallingbostel Camp, where Heinz Lorenz turned over one of the copies of Hitler's will to his interrogators.

The original will that Lorenz had with him is now in the Imperial War Museum in London. The two copies can be found in the US National Archives in Washington DC.

Nicolaus von Below (1907–83) – Heinz Mathiesung

After his departure from the inn in Havelberg, air force assistant Nicolaus von Below travelled with a pass on a false name to Burg, near Magdeburg. There he stayed with an acquaintance. Eventually he swam across the River Elbe there. After that he found his family just in time to witness the birth of his child. On 7 January 1946 he was arrested by the British in Bad Godesberg. He ended up in an interrogation camp near Iserlohn and from there went to a camp in Bad Nenndorf. On 11 July 1946 he was transferred to a prisoner camp at Zedelgem, near Bruges, and in September he was moved again to a prisoner-of-war camp in Münster. On 30 May 1947, he was transported to Adelheide Camp, near Delmenhorst. On about 2 March 1948 he was transferred to the prison in Nuremberg where he was interrogated again. After a stay of ten weeks, he returned to Adelheide Camp. He was released on 14 May 1948. He lived in Germany for the remainder of his life.

What happened to von Below's co-worker Heinz Mathiesung is not known.

A Doctor at the Reich Chancellery

That Berlin would be defended was an important decision for all inhabitants of the city, including SS physician Ernst Günther Schenck. In the second part of April 1945 he stayed at the administrative headquarters of the SS called Unter den Eichen, where some other medical personnel were based too. Now the Soviets closed in, it was decided that the people working here would move to a location outside the city. But since Schenck had specialized in nutrition and he had access to all buildings where food and coal were stored, he hesitated.

Buses and trucks were already arriving, to transport officers and staff members to the new location but Schenck, especially now, thought that he could be of assistance to the city and its people.

To get permission to stay, he had to convince his superiors that he was more useful in Berlin than outside the city. It took Schenck some effort to persuade them, but when he succeeded, he gave his employees the choice of whether they wanted to stay with him or not. Those who stayed committed themselves to helping civilians and soldiers when the city ran out of food during a possible siege. After he had watched the cars leave the courtyard one by one, Schenck had to improvise.[2] He didn't really know what was going to happen and what his work would be in the coming days. For the time being he travelled between the SS headquarters

The building where Dr Ernst Günther Schenck was stationed until just before the end of the war.

In 1945, the offices of the Wehrmacht were still located in this Berlin school, which Schenck sometimes visited.

and the offices of the Wehrmacht. But to get anywhere quickly was quite difficult because the city's streets were almost impassable. Everywhere was smoke and dust and taking short routes sometimes took hours.[3] At one point, however, Schenck and his companion Müller came close to city centre. When they left the Potsdamer Straße they decided to drive in the direction of the Brandenburg Gate, but halfway there they passed the rear of Hitler's Chancellery and saw the garage gate was open. They decided to drive through the gate and parked the car behind the Chancellery.

When they entered the building, news soon spread and that Schenck might have access to provisions. From ministries and all kinds of organisations in the area, men turned up demanding food and a variety of other necessities. This meant that now Schenck had to make sure that supplies were brought to the Reich Chancellery. To do this he required a number of trucks and when he acquired them it took him three days to transport all the coal, food and other items that were needed in the area.[4]

Inside the Chancellery soldiers and civilians took shelter together and lay close to each other on the ground, while the lights on the ceiling danced to the rhythm of the strikes during the heavy bombing on the night of 24/25 April. The walls of the building moved, and only some of the soldiers still had helmets. During that time wounded men and women were brought to the building and its improvised hospital. To Schenck's surprise the Chancellery was still standing when the shelling finally stopped that morning.

When he had finished supplying the Chancellery, there was still much to do inside the building. As he was a doctor and because there were so many wounded there, he started to help preparing the patients that were waiting for treatment or surgery. However, since completing his training he had not been involved much with patients because he had specialized in nutrition, but he was still able to do the preparatory work very well. Werner Haase was the surgeon of the field hospital. He and two sisters tried to treat all of the wounded people that were laying in the hallways. Of course, Schenck met Haase. The surgeon told him that he had been Hitler's supervising physician until 1936, but that he stopped working for him because eventually he would have had to give up his job as a surgeon to be able to attend to Hitler full-time. But now Haase, during the last days, had heard that the Führer was without a doctor, and he had applied for the job that Dr Karl Brandt had left. However, it turned out that Dr Stumpfegger had already filled the vacancy. Hitler then asked him to lead the military hospital of the Reich Chancellery which had no doctor at the helm, and Haase agreed to that. Within a few days the hospital had become so busy that he was glad Schenck had offered his services.[5]

Haase was ill. He had a lung disorder that tired him so that he often had to rest during the working day.[6] As a consequence, it wasn't long before he asked Schenck if he could take on some of the operations. Schenck, with little experience of operating, was shocked when Haase suggested this. He knew Haase could not carry out the operations on his own anymore and he had noticed that he sometimes had to withdraw to catch his breath or to lay down for a while, but Schenck hadn't worked in a hospital for a long time. Haase reassured him that Schenck could always come to his sleeping quarters for advice, but that did not alleviate Schenck's anxiety. In the difficult circumstances in central Berlin at the end of the war, he had no other choice, though, and after Haase helped him to get started, he quickly got better at operating on patients.

The neighbourhood was full of emergency hospitals, for instance in the ruins of the Hotel Adlon or inside the Ministry of Aviation. Everywhere randomly assembled teams of doctors and nurses improvised as well as they could. Schenck did exactly the same. If Haase was able to, he came in and gave him some advice, but if he wasn't able to attend, Schenck had to do everything on his own. Later, he

There was not much left of the Hotel Adlon after Soviet soldiers accidentally set fire to the hotel. It was only rebuilt in 1995.

estimated that from 24 April he did about 350 operations. Fortunately, there was an emergency generator at the hospital, because in the other rooms in the building the lights quite often went off. When patients died, the bodies were brought into the park behind the Chancellery, unless it was under fire, and then they were laid down right outside one of the back entrances. And although the Führerbunker was just a hundred yards away, almost no one from there visited the hospital. Haase sometimes went to the bunker, but Hitler's newly appointed doctor, Stumpfegger, never came to the hospital.[7]

White Flour

Schenck only occasionally still interfered with the food supply. But his old colleagues had disappeared into the city, so when a man, covered in a coating of white flour, entered the Chancellery, someone must have sent him directly to Schenck. He was a baker, he said, and he baked bread for everyone in his neighbourhood. But now he had run out of flour, so he could not continue his work. Schenck didn't take the man's word for it, but wanted to see for himself that there was still a functioning bakery in the centre of Berlin and he therefore asked the man to take him through the ruined streets to prove to him the bakery still existed. They moved in front of the facades of the buildings, crossed Unter den Linden and behind the boulevard, somewhere in between the burning houses, was a bakery, where some men made bread from the last flour they had. In amazement Schenck returned to the Chancellery and arranged ten bags of flour for the baker.[8]

Shaking Hands with Hitler

At the end of the war the Chancellery was continuously shelled and the concrete of the ceilings trembled every time there was even a hit nearby. Now there were about 300 patients inside the building and the work in the operating theatre became increasingly difficult. The medical instruments Schenck and the sisters had at their disposal were still sterilized, but this could only be done superficially. It had already become impossible to change the bandages of the patients they cared for.[9]

Schenck had no idea what was going on at the Führerbunker, which meant that on 29 April he wasn't aware of the fact that officers were already planning a breakout. During the night of 29/30 April that changed. Haase roused Schenck to tell him that Hitler wanted to say goodbye to him and the nurses. Schenck got up, woke up the nurses and a little later they walked through the corridors of the large building in the direction of the Old Chancellery. They passed the checkpoint with the two iron doors that blocked the entrance of the bunker. Behind it was a room with a table where generals were eating and drinking. They walked past them and came to the stairs of the Führerbunker. Down the stairs there was a room in front of Hitler's private bunker rooms, where they waited. It took a few minutes, but then the door opened and Hitler came out. He apologized that he had woken them up so late. Although Schenck had never met him in person, he saw a man who was now a shadow of the person he knew from the photographs he had seen of him. He saw the crooked back and the dull look in the eyes of the extinguished Führer.

Besides Haase, Schenck and the nurses there were many more people present, mainly from the medical staff. Dentist Blaschke's assistant Käthe Heusermann was there too and she later said that Hitler started shaking everybody's hands.[10] With his lips closed rigidly, Hitler gave Schenck a quick hand. After that he thanked the group for their good work. When one of the sisters burst into tears, Hitler didn't pay any attention to it. He turned around and went back into his room.

After the rest of the group went upstairs, Schenck and Haase stayed in the bunker for a few more hours. They ate and drank at the table where Burgdorf, Krebs, Baur and Rattenhuber were already seated. That was probably inside the Vorbunker, one level higher. The sight of the broken Führer made such an impression on Schenck that at first he could not concentrate on the conversation. A little later Eva Braun and Hitler's secretaries came to the table. Schenck now woke up from his musings and heard someone whisper that Braun had just become Mrs Hitler. At about dawn Schenck went back upstairs to go to work again. In the course of the day the tired Haase also came back. He took Schenck and the sisters apart to tell them that Hitler was dead.[11]

Werner Haase (1900–50)

Dr Werner Haase handed the hospital and his patients over to the Soviet army on 2 May 1945, when he was arrested himself. Because Haase had been Hitler's doctor, he ended up in Butyra Prison in Moscow. According to a Russian source, he died there in November 1950.[12]

Chapter 6

The Great Escape from the Führerbunker

After all the bombing, shelling and fighting, Berlin was a mess. Historic buildings had collapsed, Hitler's New Reich Chancellery was full of holes, churches had lost towers, stations had been razed to the ground and entire city blocks had been crushed. There were soldiers fighting everywhere – in streets, in cemeteries, in government buildings, at airports. In the beautiful Gendarmenmarkt no building was left undamaged. Even the Berlin Zoo was ruined. Of the 1,600 animals resident there on 1 April, only 91 were left by 31 May 1945.[1] The residents of Berlin had fled, sought shelter in a cellar, a bunker or in a U-Bahn tunnel or hid in their homes, if they still had one. Through that chaos, before the weapons were finally laid down, a large group of fugitives that remained in the Reich Chancellery finally planned their escape from Berlin.

Secretary Junge was one of them. She had overheard a conversation between Günsche and Mohnke about the escape attempt. Together with Mrs Christian, they asked if they could be included. Junge estimated that the chances of getting out alive were small, but anything was better than staying inside the bunker, which for her felt the same as committing suicide.[2] Of course the men agreed, but it would be a dangerous trip. While the escape plans were being discussed, Junge waited with the others who were not directly involved in the preparations. It took until late in the evening on 1 April, more than a day after Hitler's death, before the first group left the building. General Weidling, who was responsible for the negotiations about the capitulation of the city, had promised that he would try to slow the negotiations down as much as he could, but at least until it became light. That gave the escapees enough time to get to the north, he thought.

The evening before the escape Mohnke informed the officers inside the Vorbunker of the true situation. Hitler was dead, he said, just like Goebbels, and the negotiations with the Soviets had failed.[3] It was high time to go. Günsche picked up the secretaries together with Hitler's cook Manziarly and brought them from the bunker to a coal cellar under the New Reich Chancellery. There a large group of fugitives had gathered. Junge recognized Bormann, Baur, Stumpfegger, Kempka, Mohnke, Hewel and Admiral Voß.[4]

The escapees were divided into groups that would leave the site intermittently. It is not clear how many groups were involved, though some reports mention ten

The Kaiser-Wilhelm-Gedächniskirche is a reminder of the destructive power of war. Of the original church, only the battered tower remains.

groups of twenty men.[5] Other sources list just six or three groups.[6] In practice it made little difference.[7] If, in this tense situation, the groups kept to the agreed departure scheme, they would still overtake each other or lose group members. People who escaped together lost contact in no time at all, after which they joined other groups or went further on their own. It was pitch-black and crowded in the corridors of the U-Bahn, houses in the streets above it were burned down, crossings were often impassable and bullets could be expected from every corner. It was impossible to maintain radio contact. This chaotic situation later resulted in conflicting accounts from the witnesses who were involved in the escape. In these extremely stressful final days of the Third Reich everyone was concerned with his own survival. It didn't matter what time it was exactly, what the number of the house was where someone sought shelter or how big someone's group had been 2 minutes earlier.

At this late hour, large numbers of people left the area surrounding the Reich Chancellery too, mostly from other government buildings. Some sources state that as many as 2,000 people emerged at the same time as the escape groups from the Chancellery, as well as General Mohnke's soldiers with tanks.[8]

It was the intention that each group would go to the north, because other routes were far too dangerous by this point. Through the U-Bahn tunnel, which had an entrance at the Wilhelmplatz in front of the Old Chancellery, they would go to Friedrichstraße station. From there they would try to get over to the other side of the River Spree. Whether they could take the U-Bahn tunnel there or the bridge over the river had to be decided on arrival. If they succeeded in getting behind the Spree, they were to travel further north, from Stettiner station to Berlin-Tegel, if that was still possible. From there they had to aim to reach the German troops in the north-western parts of the city.

The First Group

The first group that left the New Chancellery consisted of Wilhelm Mohnke, Otto Günsche, Walther Hewel, Hans-Erich Voß, Gerda Christian, Traudle Junge, Else Krüger, Constanze Manziarly, Ernst Günther Schenck and a large group of soldiers and members of Hitler's bodyguard. Their estimated departure time was between 2200 and 2300 hours.

Secretary Traudle Junge was sat with the other secretaries and Hitler's cook Manziarly in the coal cellar of the Reich Chancellery. Junge had only brought some cigarettes and a few pictures, but some others quickly filled their pockets with all kinds of 'important' things. Almost everyone had destroyed their identity papers. Everyone was waiting for the moment the first group would leave.[9] It must have been about 2200 hours when adjutant Schwägermann came in with a chamberlain. He told them that a few minutes earlier Goebbels and his wife had committed suicide.[10]

It took courage to go first, because no one knew exactly what was happening on the outside, not even those who sometimes left the Chancellery grounds. The situation changed too often and too fast for anyone to be able to make predictions. Mohnke

The extension of the Old Reich Chancellery on the Wilhelmstraße, with the Führer balcony. Behind the old building next to it, is the Voßstraße from where several groups of bunker escapees crossed the road to the U-Bahn entrance on the Wilhelmplatz. (*Picture: NARA*)

had proposed that he would lead the first group together with adjutant Günsche, adjutant Voß and state secretary Hewel. He had also asked Martin Bormann to go with him, but, as Mohnke later wrote, Bormann wasn't brave enough. He let his secretary Krüger take his place while he chose to go with one of the later groups.[11] Dr Schenck, who had just said goodbye to his colleague Haase, joined the first group. Together with about a hundred of Mohnke's soldiers they finally left the New Reich Chancellery in the dying hours of 1 May.

Since the end of the war the Voßstraße has almost completely been built up again, except for this clearing which marks the spot where the first group of escapees gathered underground.

Red marble from Hitler's New Reich Chancellery was used in the rebuilding of Mohrenstraße U-Bahn station after the war.

At the end of Voßstraße is the junction with Wilhelmstraße. Here Mohnke's group had to take a gamble and cross it in order to get to the U-Bahn tunnel.

Taking the U-Bahn

Mohnke took the lead. He crawled out through a cellar window and crossed the street to the U-Bahn station. The others followed right behind him. Dr Schenck later explained that they crossed the street in groups of five or ten.[12] It could very well have been that those who were still in the bunker decided to override the agreed interval of 20 minutes between groups departing when they saw or heard that the first group had successfully crossed the Wilhelmstraße.

Carefully moving along the broken steps, Mohnke and his group entered the dark platform of the underground. There they were anything but alone. Many civilians and soldiers were hiding there below ground. Mohnke was looking for the railway tunnel to the north, but it was so crowded that the group had already started to break up when he jumped off the platform and entered the tunnel. Schenck was asked to keep an eye on the four women and he did his best to stay with the men in front while checking if the women were still following behind.

Carefully, the first group entered the U-Bahn tunnel.

The entrance to the U-Bahn tunnel, which would have been crowded with many civilians taking shelter, as well as groups of soldiers.

From one of the tunnels of Friedrichstraße station Mohnke's group went up into the station building.

The Weidendammer Brücke from the U-Bahn stairwell.

The first group decided not to take the Weidendammer bridge to freedom, but the train bridge right next to it.

Almost all the glass roof of the old Friedrichstraße station was broken during the war. The station has been renovated several times since then.

When they reached Stadtmitte station, a little bit of light there made it possible to form a smaller group of the twenty or so men and women who had managed to keep up. With this smaller group Mohnke entered another tunnel, which led to Friedrichstraße station. This was the last station before the Weidendammer Brücke over the River Spree.

Moving with this smaller group was much easier. Everyone managed to follow quickly and it didn't take long before they saw some faint light at the end of the tunnel. It had to be the light of the station they were heading to, but since they knew the Soviet army was on the other side of the river, they had to take great care. With their weapons at the ready, three men went ahead to check if the station and the stairway were clear. In the dark of the tunnel the others waited anxiously. Luckily, the signal was soon given that the coast was clear.

The rest of the group crawled onto the platform and entered the station building. It looked as if no one was out on the streets, but Schenck heard someone say that they should not venture outside because it was very dangerous to go near the Weidendammer Brücke. In the distance he could see the city burning. 'We're taking the railroad bridge over the Spree,' he heard someone shout. He looked around the corner and saw that the railway bridge was still intact. Friedrichstraße station was not only a U-Bahn station but also a junction for above-ground trains. The railroad track ran more than 10ft above the ground from Friedrichstraße station to Lehrter station, but it first crossed the river over a bridge. On the other side the tracks ran over a dam that went in between the houses and remained above street level until reaching Lehrter station. Schenck observed that the glass roof of the station was completely shattered.[13]

Over the Railway Bridge

To get to the railway bridge Mohnke took his group along the wall of the station to a narrow staircase leading to the track. Before they could go up, they had to remove barbed wire that was twisted around the railings of the stairs to keep the route closed in both directions. The railway bridge itself was also blocked with barriers and barbed wire. Stooping, they tried to get to the other side of the river before the Russians noticed them. When they reached the other side, they took the first small staircase to the Schiffbauerdamm, from where Mohnke wanted to pass through the city quarter of Charité.

But first they took a moment to gather themselves in a cellar on the Schiffbauerdamm. They had made the right choice. The U-Bahn tunnel that ran under the river had been closed by a Berlin traffic company and if they had made it across the Weidendammer Brücke, they wouldn't have got much further than a

After making their way through blocked stairs, the group arrived at the railway bridge.

The railway still runs between the houses on the other side. In 1945, Soviet fire threatened from all directions.

few blocks. On both the bridge and the street there were tank barriers. Behind the second barrier was the Soviet army. The Russians weren't shooting yet, but they would soon be alarmed by all the German activity near the bridge.

It was 0200 hours by the time Mohnke's group was on the move again. The district across the street was largely destroyed, so they slowly picked their way through the rubble, cellars and courtyards to find a way out. Evading the Russians, they finally reached Invalidenstraße, where they walked past the Museum of Physics to the junction with the Chausseestraße. To the right the street was still called Friedrichstraße and went back to the Weidendammer Brücke. By now they could hear that the Soviets had already taken the bridge under heavy fire.

Mohnke, of course, went in the opposite direction of the bridge, to the north side of town. Passing in front of the facades of the houses, they arrived at the main entrance of the Maikäferkazerne, near today's Habersaathstraße. Here German men of the Volkssturm civilian army had created a blockade. The men had long since disappeared, but Mohnke saw a Soviet tank behind the roadblock. He and some of his soldiers made a frantic attempt to disable the tank, but they failed. There was no way of getting through the blockade and they decided to go back to the Invalidenstraße. They were tired and cold and sought a place to rest.

At this location, a Soviet tank blocked the passage of the group.

A Soviet tank at the German-Russian Museum, Berlin-Karlshorst.

Somewhere in between the houses they found a collapsed roof that was still on fire, where they could warm themselves a bit. They tried to rest for a while, but, despite their fatigue, most of them were unable to sleep.[14]

The Next Morning

It was about 0700 hours when everybody readied themselves to leave. Past Stettiner station along the Bernauer Straße, the tiring journey continued to the junction of the Brunnenstraße. There they headed north in the direction of Berlin-Gesundbrunnen. Along the way, they were joined by lots of German soldiers taking the same route. The shooting had ceased for a few hours and civilians came out of their houses. Some of them gave the passing soldiers a few cigarettes or something to eat or drink. Nobody in Mohnke's group knew that Weidling had already capitulated.

At Humboldthain, where one of the city's large above-ground flakbunkers was built, Mohnke, Günsche, Hewel, Schenck and the four women halted. Groups of German soldiers, including Mohnke's soldiers, gathered at the park near the bunker. While the group from the Reich Chancellery rested for a while, Mohnke approached a Tiger tank where a meeting of generals took place. Even though little was known about the situation in the rest of Berlin, they decided to lay down their weapons.

The old station where Mohnke's group passed by has been replaced by an overground metro station.

The flight continued along Bernauer Straße where there is now a well-known Berlin Wall memorial.

Berlin had three flak towers, one of which is still visible. Near this tower at Gesundbrunnen, Mohnke consulted with other generals.

The first group of escapees ended up in this brewery courtyard. What happened there featured in the famous film *Der Untergang* (2004).

Nobody later remembered why, but Mohnke left the area taking the remainder of first group of bunker refugees with him. They sought shelter two streets further along, at the Prinzenallee. There, in the courtyard of a brewery called the Schultheiß-Patzenhofer-Brauerei, many other German soldiers were hanging about, waiting to see what would happen. Civilians, including many women, had joined them. They must have felt much safer near the German soldiers than alone in a ruined city crawling with drunken Soviet soldiers.[15]

At the Brewery

Mohnke and the others retreated to the cellar of the brewery. If anybody still harboured any lingering ideas of a possible outbreak, these thoughts now fell to pieces. Soviet tanks were nearby and the Soviet units quickly surrounded the brewery.[16] There was no point in fighting anymore, but the atmosphere was so tense that Mohnke's adjutant suddenly shot himself. Several other soldiers made plans to do the same, including Mohnke. He sent a negotiator to the nearest Soviet unit and then decided it was time to end his own life. He reloaded his gun, put the barrel against his head and … then Günsche took it out of his hands. He was just in time and later in life Mohnke was grateful for this.

The old brewery building still exists.

The members of Mohnke's group retreated to the brewery's cellar.

At one point another bunker refugee, Rattenhuber, came in. He had been shot in the leg while leading one of the other groups. He had managed to get through, but he wasn't in good shape. He was delirious and he had put his loaded gun next to him, in case the Russians came in.[17]

Mohnke came to talk to the women in his group after he had finished writing something. He said that it turned out that they were the only ones that could reach Dönitz now, so he could only ask them if they would take Dönitz the message he had just composed. They had to go on their own, though, without soldiers protecting them and Junge didn't like that at all. But, like the other women, she went along with it and a little later the three secretaries and cook Manziarly walked out of the courtyard, heading west.

When Mohnke's negotiator returned, they finally surrendered. Right after that, a Soviet general came to the cellar of the brewery to talk to him. Mohnke later said that the general was quite friendly and although he had to hand over his ammunition, Mohnke was allowed to keep his gun. It still contained the bullet he had wanted to use to kill himself, but it was of no further use now.

The beer cellar was one of the last locations in Berlin where German soldiers surrendered, the Soviet general had said, and defending it was useless. When the

Germans finally heard that Weidling had already surrendered, the atmosphere among the soldiers changed and many of them stopped thinking about breaking out or committing suicide.[18]

Mohnke and Günsche were taken to the staff of the Soviet army, where they received confirmation that Weidling had indeed surrendered. Then they were taken back to the cellar, where most of the soldiers had given themselves up. Schenck and Hewel and some other men were still hiding in a room, though. When Mohnke found them, he explained that it was better for them to surrender, but when some Russians came in behind Mohnke, Hewel grabbed his gun and shot himself in the head. The rest of the men were taken away by the Soviets.[19]

Wilhelm Mohnke (1911–2001)

General of the Waffen SS Wilhelm Mohnke and his staff reported to the Soviet General Chuikov after his surrender in the cellar. The following morning he was transported to Strausberg and then taken to Moscow by plane, where he was locked up inside Lubyanka Prison. After that, he spent most of his captivity at the Woikowo Prisoner-of-War Camp. In October 1955 he was released and he returned to Germany. In Hamburg he worked as a car salesman. At the end of his life, he lived on the coast in the northernmost part of the country. He spoke little about the period he spent in Russia.

Otto Günsche (1917–2003)

Hitler's personal adjutant Otto Günsche ended up in the Soviet Union in 1945 and in 1950 he was sentenced to twenty-five years' forced labour. In 1955, however, he was transferred to the Bautzen disciplinary house in the GDR. When he was released in 1956, he left for West Germany, where he worked as a manager near Cologne.

Ernst Günther Schenck (1904–98)

SS physician Ernst Günther Schenck gained some fame through the film *Der Untergang* in 2004. He was portrayed as someone who counterbalanced fanatical Nazis. That may have been true for that period, but Schenck had, for example, also been in charge of a plantation near the Dachau Concentration Camp where more than a hundred forced labourers died.[20] Schenck was arrested at the brewery and detained in the Soviet Union until the mid-1950s. He then went back to West Germany and worked in the pharmaceutical industry.

Johann Rattenhuber (1897–1957)

The leader of Hitler's Security Command, Johann Rattenhuber was also arrested at the brewery. He was taken to Moscow and stayed in various prisons in the Soviet Union. On 15 February 1952 he was sentenced to twenty-five years' imprisonment, but he was released on 10 October 1955. He was handed over to the GDR, which allowed him to go to West Germany. He died in Munich.

Gertraud 'Traudl' Junge (1920–2002)

After her return to Berlin, Junge ended up in a cell at this location on Marienstraße.

During her journey to escape Berlin, Hitler's secretary Traudl Junge lost contact with the other three women, after which she joined the long stream of refugees heading north-west. When she arrived at the Elbe she didn't dare to swim across and decided to go back to Berlin. On 9 June 1945 she was arrested at the house of a Berlin friend she had met during her flight. Someone probably betrayed her. She then ended up in a group cell inside a cellar of the Rudolf-Virchow Institute. After that she was transferred to a prison cell in the Berlin headquarters of the Soviet commander in the Marienstraße. There, an Armenian interpreter looked after and protected her, and he arranged work and a place for her to live. In April 1946 Junge managed to return to Bavaria.

Constanze Manziarly (1920–45)

Hitler's cook Constanze Manziarly left the brewery with the three secretaries. While two of the secretaries lined up to fetch water somewhere, Manziarly tried to exchange her army coat for an ordinary one. A little later Junge saw her in between two Soviet soldiers. Manziarly shouted that they wanted to see her papers. After that, Junge never saw her again. Manziarly has been considered missing since this time. Some sources say she committed suicide.

Gerda Christian (1913–97)

Secretary Gerda Christian fled to Bavaria, but was arrested there and interrogated by the American military police. For a period of time, she joined a political movement, striving for the recovery of National Socialism. For a large part of her post-war life she lived in Düsseldorf.

Else Krüger (1915–2005)

Bormann's secretary Krüger was arrested and interrogated by the British during her flight. She married her interrogator Leslie James and went to live in Wallasey, Great Britain.

The Other Groups

The organization of the subsequent groups was even less orderly than that of the first one. The group led by the head of Hitler's Security Command Johann Rattenhuber probably left first. He went together with Hitler's pilot Hans Baur, second pilot Georg Betz and a member of Hitler's bodyguard, Peter Högl. Artur Axmann is said to have left at about the same time with a group of roughly 200 members of the Hitler Youth. The group of State Secretary Naumann probably left the Reich Chancellery soon after that. Bormann, a group of party members of the NSDAP and a battalion of the Berlin People's Army joined Naumann, as did pilot Hans Baur and Dr Ludwig Stumpfegger. Driver Kempka and chamberlain Linge seem to have left together, with some staff, guards and drivers from the bunker. Hitler's naval aide Alwin-Broder Albrecht was supposed to lead another group, but he probably committed suicide before the escape took place.[21] The estimated departure time of the Rattenhuber group was about 2230 hours at the earliest, but most likely after 2300 hours.

Departure

In the early months after the end of the war almost nothing was known about the escape from Hitler's bunker. Witnesses had died, disappeared or weren't heard of as yet and, of course, nobody had had the time to write a book about it. Historians depended on the accounts of eyewitnesses, but even when they started talking

Arthur Axmann left with a group of Hitler Youth boys in the direction of boulevard Unter den Linden.

Axmann said he had seen Soviet soldiers near the Brandenburg Gate.

there weren't many reports concerning members of the Rattenhuber group. It was different for Axmann's group because Axmann wrote about the escape himself. He recounted that he left his headquarters at the Wilhelmstraße together with his staff and a large group of Hitler Youth boys. The headquarters were located exactly between Unter den Linden and the U-Bahn entrance on the Wilhelmplatz and it would be quicker if they took a route above ground directly to Unter den Linden instead of the route through the U-Bahn. Carefully, he and his boys moved along the Wilhelmstraße in the direction of the junction with the boulevard. There the route became dangerous because the crossing was only 650ft from the Brandenburg Gate. Behind the gate was the Reichstag, which was an important target for the Russians. Axmann said he saw Soviet soldiers camping near the Brandenburg Gate and that there were Soviet guns and tanks in the area. In the city filled with the sound of explosions and rattling machine guns, a large group of boys followed him quietly along the boulevard to the Friedrichstraße. It was only there that the chaos really erupted, Axmann described. The street was full of soldiers, civilians, ambulances and everyone wanted to go north. When they arrived at the Weidendammer Brücke, German tanks were already breaking through the barrier on the bridge.[22]

Kempka and Linge might have arrived at the Friedrichstraße at about the same time. They had left the Chancellery through a cellar window and cleared the first

In contrast to this picture, it was complete chaos in Friedrichstraße when Axmann arrived.

stretch through the U-Bahn tunnel too. Linge said the Friedrichstraße was already under fire. While Linge mentioned Kempka, Kempka didn't mention Linge as his companion at that time.[23]

Naumann, together with a battalion of the Volkssturm from the Ministry of Propaganda, had preceded Kempka and Linge. Naumann, with Bormann, Baur, Stumpfegger and Schwägermann, ran from the entrance of the New Reich Chancellery on the Voßstraße to the U-Bahn station on the Wilhelmplatz.[24] They had already seen that the Wilhelmstraße was still safe. Using the same damaged steps as Mohnke, they climbed down to the station platform. They too discovered it was impossible to keep an eye on each member of the group inside the gloomy tunnel. The darkness also made it difficult to choose the right way, even though the route to the Friedrichstraße was not that difficult. There was only one location where they could go wrong and that was at Stadtmitte station where they had to choose between two tunnels. And there, it did go wrong. The tunnel they took brought them to Hausvogteiplatz station instead of Friedrichstraße station. When

In the dark tunnel near Stadtmitte U-Bahn station, Naumann and Bormann's group took the wrong turn towards Hausvogteiplatz station.

The beautiful buildings of Gendarmenmarkt had taken a beating, but the square was eventually restored to its former glory after the war.

they discovered they had arrived at the wrong platform, they decided to leave the tunnel in order to find the way back to Friedrichstraße station above ground. From the ruined Gendarmenmarkt they could take different routes. Which one they chose is unknown, but between the piles of stones and burning houses they finally reached Unter den Linden. They had lost precious time, but at least Bormann, Naumann, Baur and Stumpfegger were still together. After they had crossed the boulevard it was only a short walk to the bridge.[25]

After their detour, some members of Naumann and Bormann's group reached the junction of Wihelmstraße and Friedrichstraße.

Hentschel's Bunker

In the dying hours of 1 May, there were only two men left inside the bunker – Rochus Misch and technician Johannes Henschel. Upstairs, inside the Chancellery, the doctor and his nurses were taking care of the large number of patients, but downstairs nothing was really happening. Misch was sleeping in the telephone exchange and Henschel checked his machine room. The diesel engine was still working, just like the water pump. Every once in a while, Henschel did a round of the bunker to check everything. At about 0300 hours he woke up Misch, who still had a chance to get away. Misch asked him if he was going too. He couldn't go, Hentschel said, because the emergency hospital still needed power and fresh air and it was his job to see to that. Misch must have been one of the last men to leave the New Chancellery. Everyone who had joined a group had already left the building when he went to his telephone switchboard and pulled out all the cables. He hoped to catch up with one of the groups that had left hours ago, but before he went, he had to say goodbye to his chief Schädle, who gave him the details of the route the others had taken. Misch then climbed out of a window of the Borsig Palace and crossed the Wilhelmstraße. Just before he went down the stairs to the U-Bahn tunnel, he looked back at the Chancellery one last time. His chief Schädle was still inside. It wasn't long before he committed suicide.[26]

When Misch left it was 0350 hours. Meanwhile, Hentschel went downstairs to check again. He was alone inside the bunker and he described the scene as something akin to 'a medieval crypt'. Soon he got the urge for some air. At 0900 hours, when Hentschel was doing another round through the front bunker, he heard some voices. It had to be the Russians, the technician thought. He was right, but they were women's voices and he hadn't expected that. When the Russian women entered the bunker Hentschel put his hands in the air, but they had no weapons. By their uniforms he could see they were medics. The eldest spoke fluent German, and even with a Berlin accent, Hentschel noticed. She approached him to ask who he was and what his job was. After he explained he was the bunker's technician she wanted to know where Hitler had gone. He answered truthfully that Hitler was dead, but strangely enough they were not really interested in his answer. Although the women did not know Eva Braun and could not have known that Hitler had just married her, they wanted to know where Hitler's wife's room was.

When he understood they had come to loot, and that they were especially interested in Eva's clothes, Hentschel took them to the room they wanted to see and left them there. It was really remarkable, he thought, the first Russians to enter the bunker were only interested in Eva Hitler-Braun's clothes.

An hour later a second group of Russians came to the bunker. This time they were men. Hentschel put his hands in the air again, which was necessary this time because they were soldiers. Of course, they wanted to see the bunker. When Hentschel took them downstairs, the women were just walking down the corridor from Eva's room carrying bulging bags, but the men didn't seem to care. The women passed by with not only clothes, but also rugs, bottles, vases, a gas mask and an accordion. The men were more interested in Hitler and Hentschel answered their questions. Hitler was dead, he told them, but when he explained what his role was, the officer of the group said that he was sure he would be taken to Moscow soon because Stalin definitely needed technicians.

At 1130 hours a third group of Russians came in, although they were more interested in drinking and dancing than investigating what had taken place inside the bunker. None of the men seemed to have any sense of the history being made. They seemed more happy that the war was over than the fact that they had won it. Hentschel was not interested in a party and he soon left the group. When he entered the garden, another two Soviet officers came at him with drawn pistols asking where Goebbels was. He took them to his corpse. They looked at it briefly and after that they wanted to see the bunker. At about midday, Hentschel's work in the bunker was finally over. On the Voßstraße, in front of the New Chancellery, he was pushed onto a truck that took him away.[27]

Crossing the Weidendammer Brücke

Much earlier, at the Weidendammer Brücke, the atmosphere had changed. Now that the Soviets had realized that a breakout was underway, they kept an even closer eye on the bridge and started to shoot at it. Nobody knew if Rattenhuber's group had already crossed the Spree, but when Naumann and Bormann arrived, there were dead soldiers behind the bridge and it seemed there was little chance of escaping from the city centre by crossing the bridge. When Kempka and Linge arrived, they saw that Naumann, Bormann, Schwägermann, Stumpfegger, Axmann and Georg Betz were already there. They all had made it to the bridge, but one of the most arduous parts of their journey was yet to come.

What exactly happened next has never been clarified. At one point, Hans Baur might have seen Bormann sitting on a set of small steps in front of a building on the corner of the Schiffbauerdamm and the Friedrichstraße. He had crossed the bridge. There was a dead Soviet soldier in the street in front of him, Baur said, but he didn't know how the soldier got there.[28] Baur tried to get to the corner of the Ziegelstraße, but he was driven back several times. Bormann saw him and shouted that he had better stay with him. 'I still need you', he said. 'If you let

View from the Weidendammer Brücke of Friedrichstraße station, the railway bridge and (on the right) the Schiffbauerdamm.

Here, right behind the bridge, was a tank barrier, but it was risky for the Germans to pass here because the Soviet army was so close.

yourself get shot, you're no use to anyone.' Then Bormann and Baur consulted and decided that, together with Naumann and Stumpfegger, they would try to get as far behind the river as they could. Having climbed through the ruins of a hotel at the Schiffbauerdamm, they ended up near a house on the corner of the Ziegelstraße. In that street, at about 0200 hours, they found a hiding place in a cellar full of wounded people. But only half an hour later they were back on the street because sitting there achieved nothing.

Back on Friedrichstraße, Kempka consulted with a tank commander who was now advancing on the barricade near the Ziegelstraße with the aim of breaking through. Linge would have witnessed what was going on and he described that Bormann, Naumann and Stumpfegger tried to move along in the shelter of the tank. Soon the tank was hit by an anti-tank grenade and several men that were nearby were sent flying through the air. Linge thought all three of them were dead. But others said they were still alive and, wounded or not, were hiding in a hole in the ground, right behind the barricade. Martin Bormann was said to be one of them.

Kempka had also walked alongside the tanks and temporarily lost consciousness during the explosion. When he came to, he noticed Betz near him. Betz' condition was worse, but Kempka managed to get him to dentist Käthe Häusermann, after

Baur, Bormann and a few others managed to reach Ziegelstraße, but they soon had to retreat again.

which he continued on his own. Betz didn't make it, though. He died somewhere near the bridge, just like Peter Högl, who had left the Chancellery with him.[29] Axmann, who had seen the tank pull up to the Ziegelstraße, was wounded as well. Baur, who had also been in the vicinity of the tanks, stood up dazed after the explosion, just like Naumann, Bormann and Stumpfegger.[30]

At some point, Baur stated, he, Bormann and some of the others went into a house on Ziegelstraße. When Baur heard a noise there, coming from the garden, he looked through a window at the back of the house and saw that Soviet soldiers where already there. He immediately reported this to Bormann, after which they left the house at the front. With large gaps in between them, they ran across the Ziegelstraße back to the bridge. Baur was the last one to leave but right in front of the university he had to go to ground, because the Russians were shooting at him. While the other three had probably already made it or died, Baur was still at Ziegelstraße.[31]

Baur and Kempka get Left Behind

When the shooting stopped for a while and Baur finally dared to stand up, it was already morning. He managed to get to the bridge, but Bormann had already disappeared. Baur then joined a group trying to get to Lehrter station by following

Having sought refuge in a courtyard, Baur was shot and injured. This is a courtyard in the rebuilt part of the neighbourhood.

the railway above ground as it went through the neighbourhood on the other side of the river. There Baur's attempt to break out ended. When they walked into a courtyard, they were shot at and this time Baur was hit. A bullet entered his leg and he crashed to the ground. A couple of Germans from his group dragged him into a burning house and brought him into the cellar, where they laid him on the ground. There he received basic treatment for his leg and it was splinted. He also appeared to have injuries to his chest and hand.

Baur could no longer get out. The entrance to the courtyard was still being watched by the Soviets, so leaving by that route was out of the question. Staying in the cellar, however, was problematic too. It was so hot in there due to the fire that Baur had his gun ready, in case the flames got too close to him. But it didn't get to that stage. A Soviet soldier finally entered the cellar and he, with the help of some German prisoners, took the wounded man to Invalidenstraße, where he could be taken care of.

But Baur was hardly taken care of. Instead, he was constantly interrogated because he stupidly had let it slip that he had been Hitler's personal pilot. The Russians now wanted to know everything about Hitler and his death, and because of that it was a long time before Baur was operated on. He was even lifted onto a wagon and took part in a parade of the Soviet army through Berlin, showing captured German soldiers. The Soviets celebrated their victory and showed the prisoners to the inhabitants of the city. When immediately after the march someone started questioning Baur again, he refused to answer until he had been operated on.[32]

Kempka also got left behind by the men he had been with, but there were still plenty of others who wanted to get away from the bridge. Together with a group of soldiers he tried to get to Lehrter station taking the railway bridge and the railway dam. When they had crossed the bridge, it turned out that the route was heavily shelled and they could do nothing but climb off the railway embankment. When they entered one of the cellars under the railway, they found a group of foreign women workers hiding inside. They seemed a bit suspicious, but not so much because they were German soldiers but because they were afraid of what would happen if the Russians saw their uniforms. The women told them they had to take them off quickly if they wanted to get out alive. Luckily, there were workers' clothes inside the room. Kempka and the others changed clothes, hid their uniforms and from that moment on Kempka walked around dressed as a mechanic. After he had changed, he immediately fell asleep.

When he woke up, he heard the sound of Russian voices coming from outside. Kempka peered through the door and saw the women standing between a bunch of Soviet soldiers. The women greeted them cheerfully. The woman that had helped Kempka with his clothes happened to see him standing at the door, and

Kempka hid in one of the cellars under the railway.

she immediately called him. Now Kempka had no choice. He walked towards the Soviet soldiers and before he knew it, the woman introduced him as her husband, no doubt for her own safety. The leading Soviet officer seemed in a good mood and he asked for vodka, bread and meat and wanted to share it with the foreign workers. Kempka now called the other men as well. They all ate and drank together, after which it was time for the Russians to move on. When they had left, the men burned their personal papers and decided to split up. As a group they would attract too much attention, they thought. Alone they had a better chance of getting out of the city.

Kempka was the first one to leave, but he didn't get very far because around the corner he bumped into the same group of Soviet soldiers, who were just about to go back the way Kempka had come. In order to prevent suspicion, Kempka escorted them back to the cellar, where his brand-new wife was still present. The Russians now decided to throw a victory party with a lot of vodka, which meant that Kempka couldn't go anywhere for the next few hours. As one of the highlights he danced with his 'wife' for the Soviet soldiers.

When the soldiers finally left, the woman offered to help Kempka get away. Together they had a better chance of getting past the Soviet checkpoints, so at every checkpoint she told the Russians she was married to him. Near Tegel they said goodbye and Kempka continued walking until he arrived at Wittenberg at the end of May. There he swam across the Elbe. After that, he immediately headed for his real wife in Berchtesgaden.[33]

Linge and Misch go Underground

Misch was the last man to leave the Chancellery but he managed to reach Friedrichstraße station very quickly. At the time he arrived, Baur and Kempka had not yet been captured, but were still on the other side of the Weidendammer Brücke, and soon they would be trying to get back. Misch did run into Heinz Linge who had not crossed the bridge. Linge thought it would be better to take the U-Bahn tunnel instead and about twenty other men had said they wanted to go with him. Maybe they could force a hatch in the panel that closed it off. If they succeeded, they thought it would be possible to get past the Russian lines. Misch decided to go with them.

Heinz Linge and Rochus Misch managed to get behind the river through this U-Bahn tunnel.

Somewhere in this area, Linge and Misch climbed out of the tunnel and were arrested.

Arriving at the large hatch into the U-Bahn, they didn't even have to make a hole because there was one already in it, most likely made by other men who had tried to get through. And better still, there were no Russians on the other side, so they could climb through and follow the tunnel north.

Further into the U-Bahn things became more challenging. At one point their passage was blocked because Soviet soldiers threw hand grenades through a hole in the roof. Some men did not want to take this risk and dropped out, but Linge and Misch, relying on their good luck, waited for an explosion and then started running, hoping the next grenade would not explode too soon. Both men, and possibly a few others, got through alive and after that managed to get almost as far as Seestraße in Berlin-Wedding, about as far as Mohnke had come. Then voices were heard along the staircase of a ventilation shaft. German voices. One of the soldiers who was with Linge and Misch climbed straight up the stairs. Misch and Linge were the last ones to follow. Misch went first but when he hopefully stuck his head out of the hole, he immediately felt a rifle butt in his back. He was forced to climb out. Then Linge followed. Both important witnesses of what happened inside the Führerbunker were captured now. The voices they had heard were indeed German, but the Germans were accompanied by Soviet soldiers. Linge and Misch had been framed by defectors or by German prisoners of war who were pressurized into helping their captors.[34]

The Death of Martin Bormann

Earlier, at the Weidendammer Brücke, a group of six well-known men from the bunker had started their final attempt to get through the Soviet encirclement. They were Naumann, Bormann, Stumpfegger, Schwägermann, Axmann and his adjutant Gerhard Weltzin. They had returned to Friedrichstraße station and they wanted to cross the railway bridge and the railway embankment through the Charité quarter to get to Lehrter station. For the Soviet snipers it was easy shooting from the houses around the railway line and anyone who wanted to get through this way must have realized that. But the men had no choice if they really wanted a chance to escape from Berlin. Across the bridge that was still blocked with barbed wire and other obstructions, they managed to get to the other side of the river. After that, they followed the dam through the city quarter and surprisingly got through until the point where the railway came out from between the houses. There the dam ran into another bridge that went over a water basin of the Spree. The men could see Lehrter station, but they still had to cross the second bridge.

They succeeded in doing so, but after that they still weren't safe. When they climbed off the track and stepped on the Friedrich-List Ufer on the other side of the basin, a group of Soviet soldiers that could not be seen from above spied them. There was no escaping. The Russians came right at them, but they were not hostile.

Bormann and five others also tried to cross the railway bridge and planned to continue to follow the track after that.

The railway bridge ended at Lehrter station, which was damaged and torn down after the war. The modern Hauptbahnhof opened in 2006.

They had probably encountered many German soldiers that had surrendered to them that day. One of them, according to Axmann, in broken German, said things like 'Chitler kaputt, Krieg aus' to let them know there was no point fighting anymore. They made no attempt to arrest the Germans they had come across because they had no idea who they were dealing with. Axmann's prosthetic arm received special attention from the enemy soldiers. They looked at it with admiration and curiosity. But although the Russians were friendly and handed out cigarettes, Bormann became very nervous.

Undoubtedly aware of the fact that he was an important catch, Bormann urged his comrade Stumpfegger to walk away with him. Stumfegger agreed and thus the two men slowly moved away from the group, leaving their comrades behind. Of course, the Russians noticed, especially when the two increased their speed as they got closer to the corner of the street. But the other German men stayed with them and shrugged their shoulders as if to say that they didn't know where the other two were going and as if they didn't care either. Bormann and Stumpfegger then turned right at Invalidenstraße, heading east.

Of course, the others wanted to leave too, but felt it was unwise to follow their comrades immediately. They stayed with the Russians for a while and when they thought they could, slowly walked away. When they arrived at Invalidenstraße the four men turned left, and went to the west side of the city, in the opposite direction to Bormann. At first, two of them walked on one side and the other two on the other side of the street until Axmann saw Naumann and Schwägermann disappear

From the old station, the men climbed onto this bank to find themselves face to face with Soviet soldiers.

between the trees. He and his adjutant continued to follow the road, though. After a few minutes, they heard the sound of tanks coming from the area of the courthouse. They quickly turned around, but it was too late. While bullets followed them, they ran back to the traffic bridge at Invalidenstraße in the station area.

When they were almost on the other side of the bridge, they saw something on the ground that looked like human bodies. When they came near, they saw the corpses of Bormann and Stumpfegger. Axmann knelt down and shook Bormann's

Of the four remaining men, two walked on one side of this road, Invalidenstraße, and two on the other side.

The bodies of Bormann and Stumpfegger lay on the old version of this bridge.

body. There was no reaction, although he could see no injuries. Whether Bormann had bitten through a poison capsule, Axmann could not say either. There was too much gunpowder in the air to smell it and because the bullets were flying around their heads, they had to get away as quickly as possible. They left the corpses behind and ran to the corner of Heidestraße where they took cover.

Weltzin gets Arrested

When things finally calmed down, they walked further into the Heidestraße and ended up somewhere in the Westhaven industrial area where they spent the night at a power station. The next morning, they acquired civilian clothes and tried to cross the canal to Berlin-Wedding. But since the bridge was blown up, they had to take an emergency ferry to the other side. Axmann was familiar with the district and he also knew that a colleague of his mother's lived nearby. They walked to the apartment complex where she lived, hoping she could help them. They agreed that

Axmann and Weltzin spent the night in this power station building in the Westhaven area.

Weltzin would wait at the door, while Axmann checked inside the building to see if the woman he knew was at home.

She wasn't, but a neighbour opened the door and let Axmann in, while Weltzin was still at the front door of the apartments keeping an eye out on the street. As residents of the other apartments had recognized Axmann as the leader of the Hitler Youth he couldn't stay. The people wanted him out of the building as soon as possible. They feared the Soviet reaction if they found out they were hiding an important Nazi. As the Russians were all over the neighbourhood, they urged him to leave immediately and one of the inhabitants took Axmann to the back door. There he asked where Weltzin was. The man that let him out told him that Weltzin had already been captured by the Soviets.[35]

Protected by his Prosthesis

Near Seestraße Axmann saw Soviet tanks and vigilantes wearing red armbands. They were checking for suspicious figures walking around and Axmann was definitely one of them. He had to get out of the neighbourhood as fast as he could. While he was trying to get away a man on the street recognized him. Axmann was afraid he would turn him in, but he didn't and instead of that he had something

In this cemetery, Axmann took his time to think about what he would do next.

To get out of the city, Axmann and his new comrade walked down the long Staatwinkelerdamm.

very interesting to say. He told Axmann he had heard that the leader of the Hitler Youth had been killed and that he was surprised to see him walking around his neighbourhood. Axmann was glad to hear that because that meant that the Soviet army wasn't looking for him.

But still he wasn't safe. People recognized him quite easily, he knew. He had been an important national socialist and in a crowded city like Berlin there would always be someone prepared to turn him in. Axmann started walking towards Goethepark where he passed a cemetery he had often walked by when he was a boy. He thought it would be best to think of a strategy before he did anything, so he walked into the quiet graveyard to take some time to think. After a while he concluded that it would be wise to surrender, but that it would be best to do so in the west. He preferred Plön, where he thought Dönitz still was.

In the cemetery he encountered an older man. When they got chatting he discovered the man wanted to go to the north-west too. They decided to travel together and they started a walk that would soon become quite a journey. They took the long Staatwinkelerdamm along the canal and reached the edge of Haselhorst by taking a towpath. At Haselhorst they had to pass a Soviet checkpoint, but

En route, the two fleeing men passed the Spandau Citadel.

Axmann's new friend had all kinds of papers with him with which he tried to prove that they needn't be arrested. Axmann's prosthesis also worked to their advantage. A man with such a modern solution for a missing arm, couldn't be a soldier, the guards must have thought.

Through Spandau they went in the direction of Falkensee. They now had almost left the city limits, but they still ran into one checkpoint after another. Axmann was by now very tired and when they found a shed with its door open, he suggested getting some rest. The past few days must have been exhausting for him, so when it turned out that there was nothing inside but some rubbish and laundry, they used the laundry as blankets for the night. All this time Axmann had not told his new friend who he was and where he came from.

After a deep night's sleep the two men got up and headed north through the countryside. Every once in a while, they knocked on a door to ask for a glass of water and a piece of bread. Sometimes they were lucky and sometimes they were not. When they had already travelled north for a long time, they arrived near the estate of Varchentin. There, a drunken Soviet soldier directed them into a loft in which he had already put some women, whom Axmann described as mentally ill. But since the soldier was under the influence, he left the door open, so Axmann and his companion could easily run away. They went west, passing the lake Müritzersee.

A Friendly Farm in Lansen

In the village of Lansen they knocked on the door of a farm to ask for something to drink. The farmer's wife was friendly and gave them a glass of milk. They got into a conversation and the farmer's wife told them that, with all the Soviet soldiers around, she worried about her daughters' safety. She also feared that her husband might be taken away because he had been a member of the Nazi Party. She therefore asked if the men could stay for the time being. There was plenty of work to do and in case of an emergency it could be useful to have a few extra men around. Axmann wondered if she would have asked the same question had she known who he was, but she did not recognize him. Both men decided to stay.

Axmann worked at the farm for a long time before being recognized. Everything changed when two young men came into the yard asking for food and a drink, just like Axmann and his companion had done themselves. These men were Estonian volunteers of the Waffen SS dressed in civilian clothes. During a meal with Axmann, one of the two recognized his voice, which he had heard before on the radio. Together with the prosthesis, he became convinced that he was having lunch with Artur Axmann, the former leader of the Hitler Youth. Axmann was lucky the men were to be trusted and the fact that the men came from Estonia was quite convenient, because they could make Axmann some false papers written in Russian, which he could use to identify himself. Since he left the Reich Chancellery

Farm buildings in Lansen, although it is unclear which farm Axmann stayed at in the village.

he didn't have any identification with him and only his companion's papers had got him through numerous Soviet checkpoints. If he made the papers complete with some kind of official stamp, he thought he was in with a chance of fooling Soviet guards if he wanted to travel again. In the nearby town of Waren, Axmann went to a Soviet office where he studied the headquarters' emblem extensively and then he asked someone to make a stamp of it out of linoleum for him. When he put the stamp on his false papers, they still looked cheap, but they were better than nothing.

Back to Berlin

In September 1945 Axmann resolved to go back to Berlin, which appears to be a rather strange decision. Axmann said that the mayor of the village, with whom he spoke regularly, had asked him if he would try to get his daughters back home. They were in the western part of the country and he would give Axmann some money to use on his way there. Axmann wasn't very clear about why he even considered undertaking this difficult task, but it could have had something to do with a person he wanted to meet behind the demarcation line between the east and west side of the country. Axmann's plan was to go to Berlin where he would conceal himself in the wagon of a train that was going west. There he would visit some acquaintances and on the way back he would try to bring the mayor's daughters with him.

But before he reached a train, he had to walk more than 90 miles back to Spandau, where he could get to the goods station through the back gardens of the houses on the Brunsbütteler Damm. When he finally got there, a German soldier who was also trying to travel to the west told him which train he should take. Together they climbed into a wagon that went to Braunschweig. On reaching his destination, Axmann got off the train and walked from Braunschweig to Gelsenkirchen, where he met the people he was looking for. Then he left for Lauenburg where he found the mayor's daughters.

One of the most exciting parts of the trip was yet to come. He had to cross the demarcation line again, but then in the opposite direction, back into the Soviet zone. This time there was no train to take him and the two young women didn't make it easy to get back unseen. At night Axmann chose to cross an open field that lay in between the western and eastern part of the country. But this time Axmann didn't succeed. Soviet guards saw and heard them halfway and took them to an office of the Soviet army. In the morning an officer came to ask where they were heading for. When it was made clear that they wanted to go east, there was no problem anymore and they were allowed to leave. Axmann then brought the girls back to their father, and after that he went back to the farm where he had been before. In November he finally left for West Germany.

When he reached Lübeck he made contact with his former colleagues, who even took him to Bavaria, where he met his mother again. A number of old acquaintances of the Hitler Youth saw to it that he received better identification papers in his false name of 'Erich Siewert'. But on his way back north again, he was arrested by Americans. They had been following him since his arrival in Lübeck because they were investigating the other former national socialists he met there. On 15 December 1945, Axmann, the most important witness of Martin Bormann's final hours, was imprisoned in a cellar in Munich.[36]

The Search for Bormann's Corpse

When the war ended, large parts of Berlin were in ruins. In between the ruins lay many of corpses – Hitler's corpse, Goebbels' corpse, those of their wives, the bodies of Goebbels' children and those of generals and patients from the Chancellery hospital. The remains of civilians and soldiers were scattered across the city. Before the clearing up and reconstruction of Berlin could begin, all the human remains had to be buried as quickly as possible to prevent all kinds of diseases spreading through the city. Two of these corpses lay on a bridge near Lehrter station, the bodies of Bormann and Stumpfegger.

For a long time, nobody seemed to know where their remains were. This resulted in all kinds of rumours circulating. Some said Bormann had already died during the tank battle near the Weidendammer Brücke and, at least, there was a grain of truth in that, because Bormann had actually been there. But others claimed that Bormann had been a spy for the Soviets and that he had fled to Moscow. Some were convinced that Bormann had ended up in South America. As his body was untraceable for a long time, the speculation persisted and has never really been eliminated since. The German author Jochen von Lang investigated the matter in a book about Bormann. According to him, Axmann and Weltzin did find the dead bodies on the traffic bridge near the station. But because Weltzin died during his imprisonment in the Soviet Union, Axmann was the only living witness who had recognized the corpse.

There were more people who had seen the bodies, though. When the Soviets had taken over the city, they ordered a lot of people to bury the corpses they found in several neighbourhoods. A number of men who worked at a post office near Lehrter station were given such an assignment. They had to bury the corpses they found in the area of the so-called ULAP-Gelände. One of the postal workers who was involved in removing the corpses of Bormann and Stumpfegger to that place was Albert Krumnov.

In 1965 Martin Bormann, together with his friend, were still officially missing and the authorities started looking for their corpses. When Krumnov was found,

The bodies of Bormann and Stumpfegger were finally found in this area.

Behind this government building, the remains of Axmann and Bormann were temporarily buried.

he was able to identify the location where he had buried them. When the digging started, nothing was found, although Krumnov had pointed out the same location that authorities had mentioned in a 1945 letter to Stumpfegger's wife Gertrud about the death of her husband.

It was not until 1972 that the remains of Bormann and Stumpfegger were discovered. During preparations for the construction of a new institute on the ULAP-Gelände, they were found about 13 to 16yd from the site identified by Krumnov previously. The diagram of Bormann's teeth from his dentist Hugo Blaschke still existed and it matched the teeth that where found. Dental technician Fritz Echtman and Blaschke's assistant Käthe Heusermann also recognized Bormann's teeth. After the investigation, the remains of both men were reburied inside the garden of a government building on the Lentzeallee. Years later, in 1998, DNA analysis was carried out which also confirmed that the remains were Bormann's. In 1999 Martin Bormann's ashes were scattered in the sea in the Kieler Bocht, outside German waters.[37]

Johan Peter (Hans) Baur (1897–1993)

Hitler's pilot Hans Baur was arrested by the Soviet army on 2 May and ended up in a military hospital in Posen. There his leg was amputated. Later he was detained in several camps in the Soviet Union and in Lubyanka Prison in Moscow. He did not serve his twenty-five-year prison sentence imposed in 1950 and returned to Germany in 1955.

Rochus Misch (1917–2013)

The small group of captured German soldiers which Hitler's telephone operator Rochus Misch had belonged to was taken on foot to Wartenberg, where the men were told to board a train. They were taken to a prison camp in Landsberg an der Warthe. From there Misch was taken to Posen, where he met Hans Baur. As Baur needed care, he was allowed to choose an escort. He selected Misch. They were not transferred to a military hospital, though, but to the Boutyrkage Prison in Moscow. They had to go to Lubyanka Prison for interrogation. There, both Baur and Misch were severely beaten during questioning. In 1946, just like Baur, Linge and Günsche, Misch was brought back to Germany, where he had to testify during the Nuremberg trials. After that, Misch went back to the Moscow prison and served time in several Soviet camps. At the end of 1953 Misch was released and returned to Berlin.

Johannes Hentschel (1908–82)

Technician Johannes Hentschel was captured by the Soviets and released in April 1949. He lived in West Germany until his death.

Erich Kempka (1910–75)

Hitler's driver Erich Kempka's stay with his wife was short-lived because after just a day and a half he was betrayed and arrested by the American Intelligence Service. He was locked up in a cell in Berchtesgaden. A period of interrogation and stays in internment camps followed. Kempka wrote that he found it terrible to have to answer the same questions about Hitler over and over again. At the end of June 1946, Kempka was brought to Nuremberg where his interrogators found it striking that he, as a simple driver, knew so much about what had happened inside the bunker. In his book, Kempka wrote that this really wasn't that strange because the others who had witnessed Hitler's death were dead themselves or trapped in the Soviet Union for many years. They were just not available to testify. After the Nuremberg trials, Kempka stayed in Camp Langwasser and after that in Camp Regensburg. He was released at the end of 1947.

Gerhard Weltzin

Axmann's adjutant Gerhard Weltzin was never heard of again. He is believed to have died in Russian captivity.

Heinz Linge (1913–80)

Hitler's chamberlain Heinz Linge was imprisoned in Lubyanka Prison in 1945, after he had been arrested with Rochus Misch. Linge was sentenced to twenty-five years' forced labour in 1950, but he was pardoned in 1955, like many of the other inhabitants of the bunker and high-ranking party members. He was allowed to return to Germany and worked as a representative for a company in northern Germany.

Werner Naumann (1909–82)

State Secretary of Propaganda Werner Naumann remained free after he disappeared in the bushes on Invalidenstraße. For a while, he worked under a false name at a farm in the Soviet occupation zone. After that he left for southern Germany. In 1950 he was granted amnesty and after that he worked for a company in Düsseldorf under his own name again. He was an important member of the so-called Naumann-Kreise, a group with political influence that aimed to rehabilitate its members and national socialism itself. Naumann was briefly detained in 1953, but he was not sentenced because he hadn't done anything punishable under German law. He later went to work for the Quandt group and lived at Gut Erlenhof near Lüdenscheid.

Günther Schwägermann (1915–?)

Goebbels' adjutant Günther Schwägermann managed to escape from Berlin and ended up in the West. He was imprisoned in the American sector from 1945 to 1947. Later he lived in northern Germany.

Artur Axmann (1913–96)

The leader of the Hitler Youth, Artur Axmann was taken to the Oberursel interrogation camp through Nürberg and Würzburg after his arrest. For weeks he was locked up in an isolation cell, which he only left to be questioned. In October 1946 he was transferred to the Civilian Internment Camp Staumühle, at Camp 4 of this interrogation camp near Paderborn. He would never testify during the main trial in Nuremberg, but the Americans did take him to Nuremberg on 3 July 1947. There he was questioned about his role and that of others during the Third Reich. On 12 April 1948, he returned to Staumühle. After six weeks' imprisonment inside the camp there was talk of him having to appear before court and because of that he went to an internment camp in Nuremberg-Langwasser. In anticipation of his case in March 1949, he was allowed to roam freely around Nuremberg. Letters in which people expressed their indignation about the release of the leader of the Hitler Youth appeared in various newspapers, until the case came to court on 21 April 1949. Axmann was, in addition to a number of other measures, sentenced to three years' imprisonment. After his release he took over a coffee company in North Rhine-Westphalia. In the 1970s he lived in Gran Canaria for about five years. After that he returned to Berlin where he wrote at least two books about his role as leader of the Hitler Youth.

Käthe Heusermann (1909–95) – Fritz Echtman (1913–83)

The assistant of dentist Blaschke, Käthe Heusermann fled the bunker with one of the escape groups. She chose her own path, though, and went back to her apartment in Berlin on 2 May. Together with dental technician Fritz Echtman, she was arrested by the Soviets on 11 May 1945. Both of them helped to identify Hitler's teeth and later they helped to describe Bormann's teeth. Heusermann and Echtman were imprisoned in the Soviet Union until 1953. After that Heusermann lived for a long time in Düsseldorf. Echtman lived in Berlin.

Helmuth Otto Ludwig Weidling (1891–1955)

General Helmuth Weidling was arrested immediately after the capitulation of Berlin. The Soviets brought him to their own country. After he had been in two different prisons in Moscow, he was sentenced to twenty-five years' imprisonment in 1952. In 1955 he died in Wladimirowka Prison in Wladimir.

Helmut Kunz (1910–76)

Helmut Kunz was the SS dentist who anaesthetized the Goebbels' children before they were killed. During interrogations in the Soviet Union, he claimed that he had given the children a syringe of morphine after which Mrs Goebbels and Dr Stumpfegger let them bite through cyanide capsules. Kunz was still present in the vicinity of the bunker on 2 May when the Soviet army entered the site. He remained imprisoned until 1955.

Fritz Tornow (1924–late 1990s)

Hitler's dog trainer Fritz Tornow, who poisoned Hitler's dog and shot her puppies, stayed near the Führerbunker until 2 May 1945. Tornow was also taken to the Soviet Union and ended up in the Moscow's Lubyanka Prison. In the mid-1950s he was released from Russian captivity. After that he produced dog food in West Germany.

Erna Flegel (1911–2006)

Sister Erna Flegel worked in the emergency hospital in the New Reich Chancellery until the Soviets entered the building on 2 May. She had occasionally looked after the children of Joseph and Magda Goebbels. Only she, nursing sister Liselotte Chervinska, Dr Haase and Helmut Kunz were still working at the temporary hospital when everybody had left. Flegel was arrested, but she soon went back to the Chancellery to work for another week. She lived in West Germany for the rest of her life.

Liselotte Chervinska

The other nurse who worked with Dr Haase was Liselotte Chervinska. She too was arrested by the Soviets on 2 May, but it is unknown what happened to her.

Johanna Ruf

Johanna Ruf was just 15 when she completed her nursing training and registered as a sister. By the end of the war, she was working in the hospital of the Reich Chancellery, where she continued to nurse until the end of May. After that, she was taken to Frankfurt am Oder, where she was held prisoner for two months. When she was 87 years old, a small book was published about her days at the Reich Chancellery.

Conclusion

Relations between the Eastern and Western Allies soon cooled after the war, which not only lead to an arms race of a magnitude not previously seen by the world, but also had an enormous influence on the investigation of the fate of Adolf Hitler and Martin Bormann.

Because important witnesses such as Heinz Linge and Otto Günsche, both of whom had seen Hitler's body and had been involved in burning the remains, had fallen into Russian hands, their testimonies remained unknown in the West for a long time. Just like the observations of Rochus Misch, who had also seen the dead bodies. Especially in early May 1945, no one seemed to know exactly what had happened in the Chancellery grounds, and even the Soviet interrogators continued to question witnesses about Hitler's fate.

Stalin tried to take advantage of the ambiguity by claiming that Hitler had escaped through Spain, a trick so typical of dictators that no one should have fallen for it. In any case, by employing this ruse he maintained the threat of the enemy who was the basis of his greatest success as a leader. By doing so, Stalin not only hoodwinked the Western leaders, but also retained the status of protector of his people against the terrible man he was seen to have successfully kicked out of Germany. He tried to sell the story to the West, after which, of course, the American secret service investigated the matter. This was then seized upon by people who saw it as proof of Hitler's post-war escape to South America, and not just as evidence of the secret service taking its work seriously by investigating what the leader of the Soviet Union had come up with.

Confusion about what had happened to Hitler was bound to arise. Witnesses were not only locked up in Moscow, some of them had died or disappeared. And of the many witnesses who were still there, such as Albert Speer and Hermann Göring, few had seen his corpse. The contradictory accounts that over the years became public about the last flight through Berlin and of what preceded it did not help either. But how could anyone with any knowledge of the confusing and disorderly situation after Hitler's death expect that everybody would have the same account of events?

Stalin quickly gagged his subordinates, who knew that the remains of Hitler, his wife and those of the Goebbels' family had been moved to a clinic in Berlin-Buch.

A view of the rear entrance to the Führerbunker in the garden of the Reich Chancellery taken after some demolition was undertaken by the Soviets and East German authorities. A part of the Reich Chancellery itself can be seen on the far right. (*Picture: Historic Military Press*)

Even after some of these remains ended up in Moscow, they weren't allowed to talk about it.

One of the first reports of the last few days in the bunker was written shortly after the war by British intelligence officer Hugh Trevor-Roper. He concluded, on the basis of interviews, diaries and witness statements, that Hitler had indeed committed suicide, even though Stalin claimed otherwise. Over time he added material to his frequently reprinted book as relevant people resurfaced or were released from the Soviet Union. The book eventually contained a list of people whose statements formed the basis for his book, which appeared in its first version two years after the war. The list included names such as Albert Speer, Hermann Göring, Karl Koller, Artur Axmann, Nicolaus von Below, Eckard Christian, Wilhelm Keitel and Erich Kempka.

But the absence of testimonies of the important witnesses Heinz Linge and Otto Günsche and the absence of the bodies of both Hitler and Bormann did not help to negate the theories about Hitler's 'real' fate. Stalin knew what they thought. Linge and Günsche had repeatedly been subjected to brutal interrogations in Moscow, and a report on these was specially produced for Stalin. But even after the main living witnesses to Adolf Hitler's death were released from Moscow in the mid-1950s, the conspiracies persisted. The report was not made public until sixty years after the end of the war. At that point, it indeed emerged that the German prisoners had never said Hitler was still alive, despite the physical and mental pressure exerted on them.

The story about Hitler's escape eventually became less important for the Russians. Attention shifted to the new enemy in the West, and that made it possible for the Soviet historian and journalist Lew Besymenski to investigate what had happened in Berlin and to publish books about it in the West. Initially he focused on Martin Bormann, whose body was not found until the early 1970s. But when, in 1972, the bodies of Bormann and Stumpfegger were discovered at the location where a postal worker said they had been buried in 1945, the conspiracy theories remained in circulation. After the Internet became popular in the 1990s the stories came to the fore once more never to disappear again.

However, publications that added something positive also continued to appear. In the 1990s, Anton Joachimsthaler, for example, gave a meticulous description of what the various eyewitnesses had seen in which he could only conclude that Hitler had committed suicide. Bormann was also the subject of publications, but in particular the examination of his DNA in 1998 was interesting. It proved that it was his genetic material. Hitler's remains in Moscow were re-examined in 2018, when a French team of medical scientists came to conclusion that Hitler also died in 1945.

The leaders of the three, six or ten groups that tried to flee the centre of Berlin in May 1945 all knew that Hitler was dead. He had no intention of leaving the city and that meant that anyone who wanted to leave had to wait for him to die. Sensational stories about secret tunnels that would run directly from the bunker to, for example, Tempelhof airport or to the Reichstag that Hitler would have used during his flight do not appear in the various reports about the breakout. The reason was simple – Hitler was dead and the tunnels did not exist, even though they would have been very useful for the fugitives.

But the escapees had no choice but to try and find their way through a city in ruins to discover a way out that, for many of them, no longer existed. Even Mohnke, Linge and Misch, who managed to pass the Weidendammer Brücke, found that eventually they were unable to get out of the city. And of those who did get away, almost everyone was eventually found and arrested.

Notes

Chapter 1
1. Ullrich, p. 552.
2. Joachimsthaler (2009), p. 110.
3. Kershaw (2005), p. 1053.
4. Linge, pp. 154–5.
5. Axmann, p. 418.
6. Kershaw (2005), p. 1055.
7. Kershaw (2005), p. 1055.
8. Misch, p. 180.
9. Joachimsthaler (2009), p. 110.
10. Misch, pp. 31–2 etc.
11. Joachimsthaler (2009), p. 112.
12. Junge, pp. 185–6.
13. Joachimsthaler (2009), pp. 110 and 113.
14. Misch, pp. 181–2.
15. Kershaw (2005), p. 1057.
16. Joachimsthaler (2009), p. 1059.
17. Kershaw (2005), p. 1059.
18. Joachimsthaler (2009), pp. 115–16.
19. Joachimsthaler (2009), p. 115.
20. Ullrich, p. 556.
21. Joachimsthaler (2009), p. 118.
22. Ullrich, p. 557.
23. Junge, pp. 188–9.
24. Misch, pp. 184–8.
25. Ullrich, p. 557.
26. Bundesarchiv, BArch RW 44-II.
27. Joachimsthaler (2009), pp. 125–6.
28. Ullrich, p. 558.
29. Ullrich, p. 557.
30. Joachimsthaler (2009), pp. 112–13.
31. Misch, p. 188.
32. Junge, p. 197.
33. Joachimsthaler (2009), pp. 125–8 and Kershaw (2005), pp. 1063–4.
34. Hartmann et al., pp. 267–73.
35. Kershaw (2005), pp. 1062–3.
36. Compare: Brechtken, pp. 376–7, Kershaw (2005), pp. 1062–5, Ullrich, p. 560, Joachimsthaler (2009), p. 126.

37. Joachimsthaler (2009), pp. 128–9.
38. Kershaw (2005), p. 1069 and Koller, p. 81: Kershaw says the order was given on the 24th. That's probably true. Joachimsthaler (2009), p. 132, dates the emergency order the 25th. Koller's remarks however indicate that the order was given just before midnight.
39. Joachimsthaler (2009), pp. 129–30.
40. Misch, p. 193.
41. Ullrich, p. 564.
42. Junge, pp. 204–5.
43. Ullrich, pp. 565–6, Kershaw (2005), p. 1069 and Joachimsthaler (2009), pp. 132–3.
44. Misch, p. 183.
45. Kershaw (2005), p. 1069.
46. Ullrich, p. 567.
47. Ullrich, p. 567.
48. Joachimsthaler (2009), pp. 134–5.
49. Junge, p. 206.
50. Misch, pp. 196–7.
51. Kershaw (2005), p. 1073.
52. Joachimsthaler (2009), pp. 135–6.
53. Ullrich, pp. 568–9 and Kershaw (2005), pp. 1074–6.
54. Joachimsthaler (2009), pp. 143–4 and Ullrich, p. 569.
55. Junge, pp. 211–14.
56. Wagner was also a member of the Volkssturm. He was shot in the head near Anhalter station and died. His body was never found.
57. Junge, p. 213 and Ullrich, p. 573.
58. Joachimsthaler (2009), p. 149.
59. Misch, p. 192.
60. Kershaw (2005), p. 1082.
61. Von Below, p. 418.
62. Axmann, p. 429.
63. Joachimsthaler (2009), pp. 152–3.
64. Joachimsthaler (2009), pp. 157–9.
65. Joachimsthaler (2009), pp. 162–4.
66. Kershaw (2005), p. 1084.
67. Junge, p. 215.
68. Misch, pp. 202–5.
69. Ullrich, p. 576.

Chapter 2
 1. Bahnsen and O'Donnell, p. 280.
 2. Bahnsen and O'Donnell, pp. 280 and 281.
 3. Misch, pp. 207–8.
 4. Bahnsen and O'Donnell, p. 291.
 5. Kershaw (2005), p. 1098.
 6. Charlier.
 7. Joachimsthaler (2009), p. 210 and Fischer, p. 171.
 8. Bahnsen and O'Donnell, p. 299 and Fest, *Speer*, p. 161. The eyewitness statements are not very clear about where the negotiations took place. Both locations are mentioned.

9. Kershaw (2005), p. 1099.
10. Joachimsthaler (2004), p. 278.
11. Joachimsthaler (2009), pp. 214–15.
12. Misch, pp. 209–10.
13. Kershaw (2005), pp. 1100–1.
14. Bahnsen and O'Donnell, pp. 315–16 and Fischer, p. 171.
15. Bahnsen and O'Donnell, pp. 315–16.
16. Bahnsen and O'Donnell, pp. 315–16 and Fischer, p. 171.
17. Mish, p. 213.
18. Misch, p. 257.
19. Misch, pp. 213–14. Of course, given the condition of the corpses, they must also have been set on fire in this version. This would have taken place inside the bunker itself.
20. Fischer, p. 171. Eberle and Uhl, p. 391, Otto Günsche said goodbye to Goebbels and his wife just before 2200 hours.

Chapter 3
1. Koller, pp. 40–62.
2. Koller, pp. 63–81.
3. Blum et al., pp. 32–3.
4. Knopp (2009), p. 175.
5. Koller, pp. 87–104.
6. Knopp (2009), p. 176.
7. Knopp (2009), p. 178.
8. Koller, pp. 112–31.
9. Knopp (2009), p. 178.
10. Knopp (2009), p. 178 and El-Hai, p. 14.
11. Koller, pp. 140–1.
12. Koller, pp. 105–54.
13. Koller, p. 152 and Knopp (2009), p. 181.
14. Koller, pp. 194–7.
15. Schroeder, pp. 200–52 and von Below, p. 411. Before he had left the bunker his colleague von Below had also asked him to destroy his diaries that were in the villa.
16. Joachimsthaler (2009), pp. 112 and 333. Joachimsthaler indicates that Schaub did not leave until the 26th. Schroeder, pp. 200–52.
17. Schroeder, pp. 200–52.
18. Schroeder, pp. 200–52.
19. Junge, p. 112.
20. Schroeder, pp. 200–52.
21. Koop, pp. 17–19.
22. Schroeder, p. 221.
23. Schmidt, and Joachimsthaler (2009), pp. 98, 112 and 263.
24. Joachimsthaler (2009), p. 333.
25. Raiber, p. 53.
26. Katz, pp. 344–55.
27. Peitz.
28. Smelser, p. 290.

Chapter 4

1. Keitel, pp. 196–200.
2. Keitel, p. 202.
3. Keitel, pp. 202–3.
4. Keitel, p. 203.
5. Keitel, pp. 203–6.
6. Scheurig, pp. 321–6 and Keitel, pp. 203–6.
7. Keitel, pp. 207 and 209, Turner, p. 178 and Scheurig, pp. 321–6.
8. Longerich, p. 727.
9. Longerich, pp. 727 and 272.
10. Kershaw (2005), p. 1075.
11. Longerich, pp. 728–9.
12. Turner, p. 172.
13. Turner, p. 173.
14. Turner, pp. 174–5.
15. Keitel, pp. 214 and 217.
16. Keitel, pp. 219–20 and 222 and Turner, p. 178.
17. Turner, p. 161 and Joachimsthaler (2009), p. 282.
18. Kershaw (2011), p. 405.
19. Kershaw (2011), pp. 404–5.
20. Turner, pp. 171–2.
21. Turner, p. 171.
22. Turner, p. 172.
23. Kershaw (2011), pp. 404–5.
24. Kershaw (2011), p. 406.
25. Turner, p. 167 and Scheurig, p. 328.
26. Kershaw (2011), pp. 407–8.
27. Kershaw (2011), pp. 407–8.
28. Scheurig, pp. 328 and 331.
29. Scheurig, p. 332.
30. Scheurig, p. 333.
31. Keitel, pp. 226–33.
32. Raiber, p. 29.
33. Compare, for example, Knopp (2013), from p. 218 and Raiber, from p. 28. It is not clear when they left. Other authors, for example, Longerich, leave it in the middle.
34. Raiber, pp. 28–37.
35. Knopp (2013), pp. 218–19.
36. Chavkin and Kalganov. In the reports of soldiers, names of places are sometimes misspelled.
37. Chavkin and Kalganov.
38. Chavkin and Kalganov.
39. Raiber, p. 32 and Chavkin and Kalganov.
40. Raiber, p. 32.
41. Raiber, pp. 34–5, Chavkin and Kalganov and Knopp (2013), pp. 218–19. Himmler eventually bites through an ampoule of cyanide in each version of the story.
42. Raiber, p. 35.

43. Chavkin and Kalganov.
44. Knopp (2013), pp. 218–19 and Capelle and Bovenkamp (2004), p. 119.
45. Bloch, Chapter 23.
46. Bloch, Chapter 23.
47. Turner, p. 168.
48. Bloch, Chapter 23.
49. Capelle and Bovenkamp (2004), p. 156.
50. Capelle and Bovenkamp (2004), p. 156 and Bloch, Chapter 23.
51. Bloch, Chapter 23.
52. Bloch, chapter 23.
53. Gellately, p. 223.
54. Bloch, Chapter 24.
55. Capelle and Bovenkamp (2011), p. 157.
56. Brechtken, p. 314.
57. Fest, *Speer*, pp. 371–2.
58. Brechtken, pp. 314–15.
59. Fest, *Speer*, p. 372.
60. Brechtken, p. 316.
61. Fest, *Speer*, pp. 373–4.
62. Brechtken, pp. 316–17.
63. Fest, *Speer*, pp. 384–5 and Brechtken, p. 319.
64. Brechtken, pp. 230 and 319.
65. Brechtken, p. 316.
66. Brechtken, p. 314 and Fest, *Speer*, pp. 370–4.
67. Brechtken, p. 321 and Fest, *Speer*, p. 389.
68. Turner, pp. 169–70.
69. Scheurig, pp. 341–2.
70. Bloch, Chapter 24.

Chapter 5

1. Freytag von Loringhoven, pp. 178–89, Boldt, pp. 175–83, Joachimsthaler (2009), p. 149, Trevor-Roper, pp. 165–8, Rothman, pp. 98–110, de Boer, pp. 260–6 and von Below, pp. 418–28.
2. Schenck, pp. 11–28.
3. Schenck, pp. 32–8.
4. Schenck, pp. 71–80.
5. Schenck, pp. 85–6.
6. Schenck, pp. 81–5.
7. Schenck, pp. 86–97.
8. Schenck, p. 105.
9. Schenck, p. 123.
10. Joachimsthaler (2004), p. 159.
11. Schenck, pp. 127–34.
12. Joachimsthaler (2004), pp. 336–7 and Schenck, pp. 147–8 mention 1945 and Vinogradov, p. 83 mentions 30 November 1950 as his date of death.

Chapter 6

1. Prenger, pp. 40 and p. 48.
2. Junge, p. 218.
3. Fest, *Der Untergang*, p. 173 and Axmann, p. 449.
4. Junge, p. 222.
5. Fest, *Der Untergang*, p. 173 and Linge, p. 170; Linge speaks of ten 'mixed' groups.
6. Eberle and Uhl, p. 390.
7. Kellerhoff, p. 75.
8. Eberle and Uhl, p. 392.
9. Junge, p. 222.
10. Eberle and Uhl, pp. 391–2.
11. Fischer, p. 174 and Eberle and Uhl, p. 392.
12. Schenck, p. 152.
13. Fischer, p. 178, Bahnsen and O'Donnell, pp. 347–50 and Schenck, pp. 152–6.
14. Fischer, p. 178, Bahnsen and O'Donnell, pp. 347–50 and Schenck, pp. 152–6.
15. Fischer, p. 178, Bahnsen and O'Donnell, pp. 350–8, Schenck, pp. 156–67 and appendix 'Weg in die Gefangenschaft'.
16. Junge, p. 223 and Eberle and Uhl, p. 393.
17. Fischer, p. 180 and Junge, pp. 223–4.
18. Fischer, p. 180 and Junge, p. 224.
19. Eberle and Uhl, p. 394.
20. Reinecke.
21. Kempka, p. 281 and Eberle and Uhl, p. 392 etc. Hitler's driver Erich Kempka later explained that the number of ten groups came from Mohnke's plan which included groups from several locations in the surroundings of the New Reich Chancellery.
22. Walters, location 617, Axmann, pp. 449–50 and Bahnsen and O'Donnell, p. 385.
23. Linge, pp. 170–1. Linge's book was published after his death. Werner Maser, who had the book published, put things in his mouth here and there. Kempka, p. 105.
24. Walters, location 617 and Baur, p. 285.
25. Bahnsen and O'Donnell, p. 376.
26. See Chapter 2, notes 16 and 17. It could be true that Misch left at 0345 hours, but if Joseph and Magda Goebbels really committed suicide 5 minutes before, it means that they died on 2 May. That's not the date commonly given for their deaths. It seems after the war there were no other witnesses around than Hentschel that could say exactly when the Goebbels died.
27. Bahnsen and O'Donnell, pp. 459–512.
28. Bahnsen and O'Donnell, p. 377 and Baur, p. 286.
29. Linge, pp. 170–1, Kempka, pp. 107–19, pp. 282–3, Baur, pp. 285–7 and Bahnsen and O'Donnell, pp. 376–80.
30. Walters, location 628 and 633. Walters mistakenly calls the station they went back to the Lehrter station.
31. Baur, p. 288.
32. Baur, pp. 288–92.
33. Kempka, pp. 110–19.
34. Linge, p. 171 and Misch, pp. 217–18.
35. Besymenski, pp. 114–30, Lang, pp. 340–2, Baur, pp. 287–96, Axmann, pp. 449–52, Bahnsen and O'Donnell, pp. 361–87 and Eberle and Uhl, pp. 388–95.
36. Axmann, pp. 451–506.
37. Koop, pp. 313–17 and Lang, pp. 343–50.

Bibliography

Axmann, Artur, *Hitlerjugend, 'das kann doch nicht das Ende sein'*, Karl Müller Verlag, Erlangen, 1999

Bahnsen, Uwe and O'Donnell, James, *Die Katakombe, das Ende in der Reichskanzlei*, Rowolt Taschenbuch Verlag, Reinbek bei Hamburg, 2004

Baur, Hans, *Mit Mächtigen zwischen Himmel und Erde*, Verlag K.W. Schütz, Coburg, 1993

Below, von, Nicolaus, *Als Hitler's Adjudant, 1937–1945*, Pour le Mérite, Selent, 1999

Besymenski, Lew, *Auf der Spuren von Martin Bormann*, Dietz Verlag, Berlin, 1965

Bloch, Michael, *Ribbentrop*, Hachette Digital, London, 2003

Blum, Katrin et al., *Das Auge des Dritten Reiches, Hitler's Kameramann und Fotograf Walter Frentz*, Deutscher Kunstverlag, München-Berlin, 2007

Boer, de, S.J., *De Hitlermythes, de feiten over de grootste mythes*, Just Publishers, Meppel, 2015

Boldt, Gerhardt, *Hitler's last days, an eye-witness account*, Pen & Sword, Barnsley, 2005

Brechtken, Magnus, *Albert Speer, een Duitse carrière*, Thomas Rap, Amsterdam, 2018

Bruppacher, Paul, *Adolf Hitler und die Geschichte des NSDAP, Eine Chronik, Teil 2, 1938–1945*, Books on Demand, Norderstedt, 2008

Capelle, Henk, van and Bovenkamp, van de, Peter, *De Berghof, het Adelaarsnest, Hitler's verborgen machtscentrum*, Verba b.v., Hoevelaken, 2003

Capelle, Henk, van and Bovenkamp, van de, Peter, *Hitler's Handlangers*, Verba b.v., Soest, 2004

Eberle, Henrik and Uhl, Matthias, *Het boek Hitler*, Bruna Uitgevers, Utrecht, 2005

Ehresmann, Andreas, *Das Stalag XB Sanbostel, Geschichte und Nachgeschichte eines Kriegsgefangenlagers*, Dölling und Galitz Verlag, München-Hamburg, 2015

El-Hai, Jack, *De Nazi en de psychiater*, De Arbeiderspers, Amsterdam-Antwerpen, 2013

Fest, Joachim, *Der Untergang*, Rowolt Taschenbuch Verlag, Reinbek bei Hamburg, 2004

Fest, Joachim, *Speer, architect van Hitler*, De Boekerij, Amsterdam, 2004

Freytag von Loringhoven, Bernd, *In the bunker with Hitler, the last witness speaks*, Phoenix, London, 2007

Fischer, Thomas, *Die Verteidigung der Reichskanzlei 1945, Kampfkommandant Mohnke berichtet*, Schild Verlag, Zweibrücken, 2008

Gellately, Robert, *Neurenberg-gesprekken, nazi's en hun psychiater Leon Goldensohn*, Meulenhoff, Amsterdam, 2004

Gottwaldt, Alfred, *Dorpmüllers Reichsbahn, die Ära des Reichsverkehrsministers Julius Dorpmüller 1920–1945*, EK-Verlag, Freiburg, 2009

Hartmann, Christian et al., *Hitler, Mein Kampf, eine kritische Edition*, Institut für Zeitgeschichte, München-Berlin, 2016

Joachimsthaler, Anton, *Hitler's einde*, Uitgeverij Omniboek, Kampen, 2009

Joachimsthaler, Anton, *Hitler's Ende*, Herbig Verlagsbuchhandlung, München, 2004

Junge, Traudl, *Tot het laatste uur*, Tirion Uitgevers B.V., Baarn, 2002

Katz, Ottmar, Prof. Dr Med., *Theo Morell, Hitler's Leibartzt, biographie*, Hestia Verlag, Bayreuth, 1982

Keitel, Wilhelm, *The memoirs of Fieldmarshal Wilhelm Keitel, chief of the German High Command, 1938–1945*, ed. Walter Gorlitz, Cooper Square Press, New York, 2000

Kellerhoff, Sven Felix, *Mythos Führerbunker*, Giebel Verlag, Berlin, 2003

Kempka, Erich, *Die letzten Tage mit Adolf Hitler*, Verlag K.W. Schütz, Coburg, 1975

Kershaw, Ian, *Hitler, Hoogmoed & Vergelding*, Spectrum, Utrecht, 2005

Kershaw, Ian, *Tot de laatste man*, Spectrum, Houten-Antwerpen, 2011

Knopf, Volker and Martens, Stefan, *Goring's Reich, Selbstinszenierungen in Carinhall*, Links Verlag, Berlin, 2006

Knopp, Guido, *Geheimen van het Derde Rijk*, Omniboek, Utrecht, 2013

Knopp, Guido, *Göring, de biografie*, Manteau/Standaard Uitgeverij, Antwerpen, 2009

Koller, Karl, *Der letzte Monat*, Ullstein, Frankfurt am Main/Berlin, 1995

Koop, Volker, *Martin Bormann, Hitler's Vollstrecker*, Böhlau Verlag, Wien-Köln-Weimar, 2012

Lang, von, Jochen, *Der Sekretär, Martin Bormann: Der Mann der Hitler beherrschte*, Herbig, München-Berlin, 1987

Linge, Heinz, *In het voetspoor van de Führer*, Uitgeverij Kadmos, Utrecht, 1985

Longerich, Peter, *Heinrich Himmler*, Oxford University Press, Oxford, 2012

Maser, Werner, *Adolf Hitler, Legende, Mythos, Wirklichkeit*, Bechtle Verlag, München, 1997

Mayo, Jonathan and Craigie, Emma, *Hitler's last day, minute by minute*, Short Books, London, 2015

Misch, Rochus, *De laatste getuige*, Fontaine Uitgevers bv, 's-Graveland, 2008

Piper, Ernst, *Alfred Rosenberg, Hitler's Chefideologe*, Cheffing, München, 2005

Prenger, Kevin, *Oorlogszone ZOO, de Berlijnse dierentuin en de Tweede Wereldoorlog*, Kevin Prenger, Amsterdam, 2015

Rothman, Herman, *Hitler's will*, The History Press, Stroud, 2014

Ruf, Johanna, *Eine Backpfeife für den kleinen Goebbels, Berlin 1945 im Tagebuch einer 15-Jährigen-die letzten und die ersten Tage*, Berlin Story Verlag, Berlin, 2017

Schenck, Ernst Günther, *Das Notlazarett unter der Reichskanzlei*, VMA-Verlag, Wiesbaden, 2000

Scheurig, Bodo, *Alfred Jodl, gehorsam und verhängnis, biographie*, Ullstein/Propyläen Verlag, Berlin, Frankfurt am Main, 1991

Schroeder, Christa, *Er war mein Chef, Aus dem Nachlaß der Sekretärin von Adolf Hitler*, Herbig, München, 2004

Ullstein/Propyläen Verlag, Berlin, Frankfurt am Main, 1991

Smelser, Ronald, *Robert Ley, Hitler's Mann an der 'Arbeitsfront', eine Biographie*, Ferdinand Schöningh, Paderborn, 1989

Trevor-Roper, Hugh, *The Last Days of Hitler*, Pan Books, London, 2002

Turner, Barry, *Karl Dönitz, De laatste dagen van het Derde Rijk*, Karakter Uitgevers, Uithoorn, 2016

Vinogradov, V.K. et al., *Hitler's Death, Russia's last great secret from the files of the KGB*, Chaucer Press, London, 2005

Ullrich, Volker, *Adolf Hitler, opkomst en ondergang*, De Arbeiderspers, Amsterdam/Antwerpen, 2018

Walters, Guy, *Naumann's War, the life of Werner Naumann from 1909 to 1945*, e-book, Lockhart Armstrong Limited, 2016

Articles and Other Material

Andreeva, Svetlana et al., Deutsch Russisches Museum Berlin Karlshorst, katalog zur Dauerausstellung, H. Heenemann, Berlin, 2014Bittmann, Julius, 'In Hinterthal war Bormanns Flucht zu Ende', in *Traunsteiner Tagblatt*, 13 March, 2010

de Boer, Sjoerd J., 'De laatste getuige, verslag van een bezoek aan Rochus Misch', in *Wereld in Oorlog*, 36, 2013

Charlier, Philippe et al., 'The remains of Adolf Hitler: A biomedical analysis and definitive identification', *European Journal of Internal Medicine*, May 2018

Chavkin, Boris and Kalganov, A.M., 'Die lezten Tage von Heinrich Himmler. Neue Dokumente aus dem Archiv des Föderalen Sicherheitsdienstes', in *Forum*, Katholische Universität Eichstätt-Ingolstadt

'Die deutsche Kapitulation in Mai 1945', Deutsch-Russisches Museum Berlin Karlshorst, Kettler, Bönen/Westfalen, 2015

'Ein sächsisches Dor fund die gefälschten Hitler-Tagebücher', website: *MDZeitreise*, 27 April 2018

Harding, Luke, 'Interview: Erna Flegel', Guardian.co.uk, 2 May 2005

'It happened here, Himmler's suicide', in *After the Battle*, No. 14, 1976

OKW/Führungsstab B (Ausenstelle OKW-Süd), Bundesarchiv, BArch RW 44-II, 1945

Peitz, Detlef, 'Gerhard Herrgesell: SS-Richter und Parlamentsstenograf. Zugleich ein Beitrag zu den Anfängen der Verwaltung des Deutschen Bundestages', in ZParl Zeitschrift für Parlamentsfragen, Vol. 45 (2014), pp. 141–57

Raiber, R., 'Fate of the Sonderzug', in *After the Battle*, No. 19, 1977

Reinecke, Stefan, 'Der Arzt von Berlin', in *Die Tageszeitung*, 15 September 2004

Schmidt, Mathias, 'Hitler's Zahnarzt. Hugo Johannes Blaschke', in *Zahnärztliche Mitteilungen*, January 2017

'Zwölf Jahre lang anständig gelebt', *Der Spiegel*, 18, 2015

Index

Index 207